THE DANGERS OF AMERICAN CHRISTIANITY

THE DANGERS OF AMERICAN CHRISTIANITY

CHRIS FRANCIS

BRIDGE
LOGOS

Newberry, FL 32669

Bridge-Logos
Newberry, FL 32669

The Dangers of American Christianity:
How Contemporary Culture Steals Our Passion For Jesus
by Chris Francis

Copyright © 2017 by Bridge-Logos

Revised First Edition

Library of Congress Catalog Card Number: 2017947788

International Standard Book Number: 978-1-61036-902-2

Cover/Interior design by Kent Jensen | knail.com

VP BP 11-01-17

ENDORSEMENTS FOR *THE DANGERS OF AMERICAN CHRISTIANITY*

"You and I want to live passionately for Christ, but if we're honest, it often feels like we're just going through the motions. The book in your hands uncovers the reasons why. Honest, engaging, and fast-moving—*The Dangers of American Christianity* is a must-read for every serious follower of Jesus. Ready to reignite your faith and leave a mark in this world for Christ? Read this book!"

—JEFF BORKOSKI, Author of Amazon #1 Bestseller *Wife Magnet*

"Francis puts a mirror in front of our collective American faces and exposes the blemishes we often ignore. Only the gospel can clear up the infection. Only the culture of the Kingdom can truly reconstruct our culture."

— BOB RICONDA, author of *The Insecure Pastor*

"*The Dangers of American Christianity* reveals how our cultural influences distort and corrupt our understanding of authentic, biblical Christianity. Written in a down-to-earth, humorous and contemporary style, this book is a manifesto for our modern times. It will cause you to think deeply about your Christian faith and grow closer to the heart of Jesus. I highly recommend this book to every Christian living in America!"

— PIERRE M. EADE, Author of *Born to Grow* and *Our Good Father*

ACKNOWLEDGEMENTS

Pierre Eade: Thank you for helping me find the passion and direction for a first book. I would still be saying, "Maybe I should write a book one day" if it wasn't for you taking an interest.

Jeff Borkoski: For 12 years you've been critiquing my projects and making them better; I'm extremely thankful for our friendship.

Bridge Logos Publishing: Thank you giving this rookie writer the opportunity.

True life church: It is because of your faithful encouragement, feedback and challenging input that I have been able to hone my communication gift. It is a pleasure to be your pastor.

Mom and dad: Thank you for the constant support on all the endeavors I've embarked on. I would not be willing to risk failure if it wasn't for the home I grew up in.

Kayla, Sienna, and Tessa: I'm more grateful to be your dad than I am to get a book published. Don't ever forget that.

The love of my life Jess: thank you for taking such great care of our three daughters and allowing me the time and space to work on this book. You're the greatest gift God has ever given me.

CHAPTER OUTLINE

INTRODUCTION

I was born with a lazy eye. Actually, it was a lazy *crossed* eye, which led to all the neighborhood kids calling me "Chris-Cross" (if you're younger than 30 or older than 55 you may not get the joke, but it was funny to the kids picking on me).

Anyway, my eye doctor once told me that I could never be in the military. As a six-year-old, that news didn't bother me. But as I grew older and began to watch war movies, I wanted to fight for my country. I remember watching "Born on the Fourth of July" with Tom Cruise and admiring the main character's patriotism, even after becoming paralyzed: "I love America. I love Americanism." It was gripping.

Later on, when I was 16, I saw "Saving Private Ryan" and was floored by the courageous sacrifice of the greatest generation who fought in World War II.

I, too, love America. I love Americanism. I love our country.

So why am I writing a book entitled, "The dangers of American Christianity"? Let me try to explain.

THE REAL THING

When Pepsi first came on the market, Coca Cola found its slogan: "The Real Thing." That was Coke. The real thing. Pepsi, it was implied, is simply an imitation.

And since then, there have been many imitations. There's the one in the 99-cent store that I used to buy when I didn't make much money. There's the one that Wal Mart sells that I buy when my not-so-important friends are coming over.

But there is only one Coca Cola. All the rest are imitations.

The same is true of Christianity. There is the real thing. And then there are imitations.

> IF CHRISTIANITY IS WORTH ANYTHING, IT MUST BE BIBLICAL CHRISTIANITY, CENTERED AROUND JESUS CHRIST AND WHAT HE IS DOING THROUGH HIS CHURCH IN THIS WORLD. BUT THERE ARE MANY WAYS IT GETS PERVERTED, TWISTED, DILUTED, AND WATERED DOWN.

And that has always been the case.

The apostle Paul tells Jesus-followers in Romans 12:2, *"Do not be conformed to this world, but be transformed by the renewal of your mind, that by testing you may discern what is the will of God, what is good and acceptable and perfect."*

And in Romans 8 he tells us that God is conforming us into the image of Christ (Rom. 8:28–29). So God is conforming us to be more like Jesus.... but we are tempted to conform to the culture's way of doing things. There is a battle going on for the formation of our hearts at all times.

In every day and age Jesus' followers have been tempted to *conform* to the cultures around them. It's not a knock on America; any culture has a tendency to do this. It's just natural that we will be tempted to value the values that the culture we live in values.

Think about it on a smaller scale: did you ever notice that the people you hang out with the most, who you like the most and respect the most, are the ones whose values you begin to adopt? For instance, take a group of friends, all in their early 20s. Let's say they are living the single new-career life, dating, going out, spending their fresh-earned money. As soon as one of them gets engaged, it won't be long before the rest begin to follow suit. And if one of them is not in a position to get engaged there will be jealousy and insecurities and maybe depression. Once one or two start getting married, the rest will, too. Once one or two start having babies, the rest will try. Did you ever notice that?

Because we naturally drift into the way of life that those around us embrace. That's normal and not necessarily bad.

But for Christians, it can be very dangerous.

In the first century the Christians in the city of Corinth were highly influenced by Greek and Roman culture, where sexual immorality and idol-worship were acceptable practices. They mixed their faith in Jesus with gross immoral sexual acts because they believed that the spirit and body were altogether separate. It was *Corinthian Christianity* and it was a perverted form of true Christianity.

When America was birthed in 1776, the Constitution was highly influenced by Christian morals and principles—and yet slavery ran rampant. And some Christians—though certainly not all—would actually use the Bible to justify it.

> BUT GOD'S WORD WASN'T TO BLAME. THAT WAS AN EXAMPLE OF SINFUL HUMANITY FILTERING THEIR INTERPRETATION OF SCRIPTURE THROUGH THEIR CULTURAL LENS.

And on and on we could go with examples.

In the following chapters we will look at specific ways that our current American culture has the potential to corrupt our faith. Ways that we either mix our faith with other beliefs, ways that we elevate good values too high, and even ways that we over-react to culture in so-called Christian ways that are really not very Jesus-like.

My hope is that this book helps you love Jesus more. And love America more. In that order.

TWO MAJOR EXTREMES

I'm writing this on November 6th 2016. Two days before the Presidential Election that has and will continue to make history.

One thing I notice as I scroll through Facebook posts and Twitter feeds is extreme side-picking sells. It's not enough to say you disagree with Donald Trump. You must showcase Donald Trump supporters as stupid and ignorant. It's not enough to disagree with Hillary. All her supporters are sold out to the Politically Correct Police.

We love drama and polarizing two sides of an issue ramps up the drama, thus making it more appealing to bite on whatever we're selling—whether it is newspapers, the prime-time news slot, or just attention on social media.

Christians are no different.

And we are certainly no different when it comes to our relationship to the culture. We love picking sides.

SYNCRETISM OR SEPARATISM

Syncretism is simply when we get too mixed up in culture. We might mix our faith in Jesus with our faith in horoscopes. We might mix our love for God with our love for money. We might mix our desire to serve other people with the desire to climb the corporate ladder at any cost.

Separatism is the other extreme. It's separating ourselves too much from culture. *I can't be around those people! They read horoscopes! They smoke! I can't let my kids hang out with those kids or they'll end up doing drugs and getting pregnant at 13.*

Biblically speaking, both are enemies of the gospel of Jesus Christ, enemies of the good news that God is offering the world. And I think it's getting harder and harder to keep from falling into either Syncretism or Separatism, because our culture is becoming more and more polarized in so many ways. Michael Wolf wrote an article in The New York magazine a few years back and in it he makes the following observation:

> *...we are at the fundamental schism in American cultural, political, and economic life. There's the quicker-growing, economically vibrant, but also more fractious and more difficult to manage, morally relativist, urban-oriented, culturally adventuresome, sexually polymorphous, and ethnically diverse nation.*

> *And there's the small-town, nuclear-family, religiously oriented, white-centric other America, which makes up for its diminishing cultural and economic force with its predictability and stability.*

Now he's stereotyping a bit but there's some truth to that. There's this greater and greater battle between traditionalists and postmodernists. Between those who hold tightly to conservative values and those who think truth is relative. The nuclear family is no longer the sacred cow it once was; no longer are sitcoms ending with Danny Tanner giving DJ a hug after she apologizes for sneaking out with Kimmy Gibler.

And many Christians are either being tempted to drift with the culture, or to run from the culture and form a little Christian bubble and then criticize the culture from within that bubble.

Often-times, we swing from one extreme to the other. We grow up in a Christian conservative home, then hit high school and swing the other way. Get into trouble and swing back. We're all about extremes.

Now why is that dangerous?

A BRIEF SUMMARY OF GOD'S PEOPLE

In the midst of a broken world full of rebellious sinful humanity, God spoke to a man named Abram who was living amongst a bunch of pagans, probably worshipping all kinds of gods. But God said to Abram:

> *"Go from your country, your people and your father's household*
> *to the land I will show you. I will make you into a great nation,*
> *and I will bless you; I will make your name great, and you*
> *will be a blessing. I will bless those who bless you, and whoever*

*curses you I will curse; and all peoples on earth will be blessed
through you."* (Genesis 12:1–3)

This word for bless means more than "favor" or good luck. It was "shalom"—everything working as it should be. All peoples: this meant all kinds of peoples, ethnicities and races and nationalities will be blessed, will be made right, through Abram and the nation God will create through him.

He trusted God and obeyed, and indeed, within a few hundred years Abram's descendants were a large people. But through a series of events, they had become slaves in Egypt. Not feeling very special. Not feeling very blessed by God. And certainly not influencing the rest of the world around them.

However, while they were slaves they multiplied and multiplied into a big nation, and then God raised up a deliverer, Moses, who led them out of Egypt and toward the Promised Land. Before he took them into the Promised Land, God made a Covenant with them: *"Now therefore, if you will indeed obey my voice and keep my covenant, you shall be my treasured possession among all peoples, for all the earth is mine; and you shall be to me a kingdom of priests and a holy nation"* (Exodus 19:5–6).

Wow, that's a huge promise. On top of the already-huge promise God had made to Abram. These former slaves are still God's plan to redeem the world.

GOD IS KING

At this point, what this nation had was a theocracy. God was King. God directly set up the government—moral, civil and ceremonial laws. And he said, "Obey me. Follow me."

Seems like a simple plan.

But Israel had a hard time obeying God. A *really* hard time.

They had a tendency to forget about God, run after the cultural practices of the nations around them, and fight with each other. The book of Judges summed it up with this: "Everyone did was right in his own eyes" (Judges 17:6).

Eventually, Israel thought the answer was to have a human king, "like all the other nations have" (1 Samuel 8:5). The apostle Paul would later write in Romans 1 that idolatry is the result of rebellion: "They exchanged the truth about God for a lie, and worshiped and served created things rather than the Creator.." (Romans 1:25). Because people refuse to worship the one true God, they look for creation—created people and created things—as their source of security and fulfillment.

Israel wanted what the other nations around them had, because they had already rejected God as their king. They said "no thanks" to the security that comes from Almighty God, and instead chose the kind of security that they saw the cultures around them trusting in.

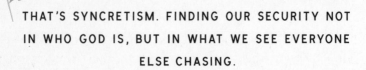

THAT'S SYNCRETISM. FINDING OUR SECURITY NOT IN WHO GOD IS, BUT IN WHAT WE SEE EVERYONE ELSE CHASING.

God granted their request, and gave them their first king—a man named Saul. Saul started off humble and "small in his own eyes" (1 Samuel 15:17); but then he, too, rebelled against God, and became more and more disobedient.

So God made David king. Despite some dark seasons and evil sins, David was a man who truly sought the Lord as the ultimate King. And God made another covenant with David:

"When your days are fulfilled and you lie down with your fathers, I will raise up your offspring after you, who shall come from your body, and I will establish his kingdom. He shall build a house for my name, and I will establish the throne of his kingdom forever. ...And your house and your kingdom shall be made sure forever before me. Your throne shall be established forever."　　(2 Samuel 7:12–13, 16).

That's another huge promise! God promised David that his throne and his kingdom would be established forever through his offspring. Pretty awesome.

After David came his son Solomon. The reign of Solomon was a time of great peace and prosperity for Israel. It was better than the 1920s were for America.

But Solomon soon drifted away from following God wholeheartedly. He went after women from other nations and his heart became highly influenced by their pagan worship. And after Solomon came his son Rehoboam, under whose reign the kingdom of Israel was divided into two kingdoms.

And for the next few hundred years, one king after another took the throne for both the northern and southern kingdoms, until finally the northern kingdom was captured by the Assyrian Empire and the southern kingdom was overtaken by the Babylonians. The temple in Jerusalem was destroyed and they were exiled.

As you can imagine, being in captivity in a foreign nation is not exactly what the people of Israel pictured when they thought of being God's treasured possession.

So now this holy nation, this special people, no longer had their own government, the temple was destroyed, and they had no influence on the world whatsoever.

Syncretism had failed them.

THE SWING INTO SEPARATISM

From around 522 BC onward, Israel was under foreign rule in one way or another: Assyria, Babylon, Persia, until eventually Rome ruled the known world. And that's when Jesus came on the scene, from the line of David, claiming to be the promised Messiah.

Now many Jews knew their history. They knew the danger of mixing in with other cultures, worshipping God along with other gods. They knew about God's promise to Abraham and Moses and David, and so there was a group known as the Dagger-bearers, who would sneak around and assassinate Roman soldiers. They made civil government extremely difficult for the Romans. They were fanatic nationalists, doing violence in the name of Israel.

They were waiting for the Messiah so they could fight back and conquer the Romans and return Israel back to the theocratic nation (one nation directly under one God) it once was and end syncretism for good.

Then there were the Pharisees—whose name meant "Separate Ones"—a highly respected group of Jewish leaders who knew the Torah inside out, were teachers of the law, and were waiting for the Messiah to take back political power as well.

But Jesus came and instead of leading political reforms, instead of rallying his troops, instead of planning a high-level assassination of all the Roman higher-ups—he hung out with known sinners, healed bodies, forgave sins, and invited people to follow him in a life of sacrifice.

And the Zealots—those dagger-bearers who wanted him to lead a revolt—well, they weren't very happy with him. The Pharisees were not happy with him, either. And they both wanted to see him killed.

JESUS—THE ANSWER TO BOTH EXTREMES

The night before he was crucified, he took bread, gave thanks and broke it, and gave it to them, saying, "This is my body given for you; do this in remembrance of me." In the same way, after the supper he took the cup, saying, "This cup is the new covenant in my blood, which is poured out for you." (Luke 22:19–20).

A New Covenant—in MY blood. What does that mean? What is he saying? What is he claiming? He's saying that through him—through his blood, his sacrifice—people can enter into all the promises that God has made for his people. God's promise to Abraham—that Israel will be blessed and then bless the world— is YES because Jesus is how all the world can enter into perfect peace with God the Father.

God's promise through Moses—that God will pour out his blessings to Israel if they obey his laws—are YES because Jesus obeyed the law perfectly on our behalf, and then took on the curses that our disobedience deserves.

And God's promise to David—that there will be a king from his line who will reign over his people forever as a Righteous King—are YES because Jesus is that King who conquered death and will live forever.

That's what he meant by this "new covenant in my blood". Through his sacrifice we can enter into the promises that God made.

The next day his blood was spilled on a Roman cross, and he died. But then he rose again, proving that He is God and that he has the power to make a NEW covenant.

And then he said to his band of Jewish followers something that would change everything: *"Peace be with you. As the Father has sent me, even so I am sending you"* (John 20:21). *As I came into this broken world, as I came as a missionary to this world, so I am sending you. Go into the world, into culture, to make disciples, to invite people into covenant with God through me.*

Jesus sent them—his disciples, this thing called the church—to fill the Earth with image-bearers who have been restored through the shed blood of Christ. And he sent them into every nation and people group, and eventually Gentiles, not just Jews, began to accept this invitation. And then there were communities of Jews and Gentiles popping up all over the place.

ALIENS IN AMERICA

Around 62 or 63 AD the apostle Peter wrote a letter—most likely from Rome—to a group of church communities that were scattered throughout Israel. In it he said:

> *But you are a chosen race, a royal priesthood, a holy nation, a people for his own possession, that you may proclaim the excellencies of him who called you out of darkness into his marvelous light. Once you were not a people, but now you are God's people; once you had not received mercy, but now you have received mercy.* (1 Peter 2:9–10)

Peter is telling these churches—filled with Gentiles and Jews—they are, together, a chosen race and a royal priesthood. Remember, God had said Israel would be a kingdom of priests, and now he's saying these Christians, this Church is the kingdom of priests. They are the royal priesthood, God's representatives to all nations. They are the ones who stand in the gap between God and destruction, the ones who are to be a blessing to the world.

They are also a holy nation. Jews and Gentiles, through Jesus, have become one holy nation. And as his holy nation, Peter tells them that they are sent into a non-God loving culture to proclaim—to declare and celebrate and point to and show off—the excellencies of the God who called us out of darkness—out of death and ignorance and false religions and a life of purposelessness—into his marvelous light, a life of purpose and grace and forgiveness and hope.

Peter continues:

"Beloved, I urge you as sojourners and exiles to abstain from the passions of the flesh, which wage war against your soul. Keep your conduct among the Gentiles honorable, so that when they speak against you as evildoers, they may see your good deeds and glorify God on the day of visitation. (1 Peter 2:11–12)

Sojourners and exiles. That could also say aliens and foreigners—those who are traveling through, who do not belong, whose home is not here. So Jesus sends us as his holy nation into every culture of the world, to influence it—but to influence it as aliens.

That includes America.

AMERICA IS NOT OUR CHRISTIAN NATION

THIS MEANS THAT AS CHRISTIANS LIVING IN AMERICA, WE ARE SENT INTO AMERICAN CULTURE TO INFLUENCE IT, BUT WE DO NOT BELONG TO AMERICA. OUR HOME IS NOT HERE.

I've heard a few debates between Christians and atheists about whether or not America is a Christian nation. And I get what Christians are saying about how Scripture played a huge role in the Constitution and Bill of Rights, especially the books of Matthew, Exodus and Isaiah. But agreeing with those morals and principles does not make a person a Christian.

To become part of God's holy people, you must go through the sacrifice of Jesus Christ. And therefore, as one blogger put very well: *"Our ultimate allegiance is pledged, not to a nation, government or political leader, but to the one true King and His kingdom—Jesus Christ. As believers ransomed from sin and death, our loyalties belong to Him. He is not interested in sharing our allegiance or affection."*

BIBLICALLY, THERE IS ONLY ONE CHRISTIAN NATION—ONE PEOPLE FOR GOD'S OWN POSSESSION, BOUGHT BY THE BLOOD OF JESUS CHRIST TO BE HIS LIGHT TO THE WORLD.

Look again at Peter's command to us. He tells us to "abstain from the passions of the flesh" (2:11). As aliens, we must resist the temptations of this foreign land. We must not value that which the culture values. That's where Israel went wrong in the early days—they mixed their worship of God with other pagan gods.

But look—"among the Gentiles..." he says. This use of the word here "Gentiles" has to do with outsiders, unbelievers, non-Jesus-followers. Peter is implying that we must have a faithful presence among the outsiders. We are to live such lives that the Gentiles are amazed at our character and love for the world.

This is what eventually flipped the Roman Empire upside down. Not because the Christians were lobbying for changes in policy regarding how the soldiers did their business or how taxes were collected. But because Christians, despite the persecution, were faithful to serve and serve and serve. To love and love and love.

And eventually people wanted to become part of this holy nation, this royal priesthood.

THREE CHALLENGING IMPLICATIONS

To sum up, let me give three specific implications that flow out of our identity as a Christian nation sent into America as aliens to live among them and influence them.

1. We Must Not Pander to and Appease the Culture

Some of us right now are trying to mix our faith with the world's ways of doing things. Maybe we're trying to make Jesus look relevant and cool to our friends. Maybe we claim to trust in God's sovereignty but seek additional insight from a fortune teller or psychic. Maybe we sing songs at church about how Jesus is everything, but our days are spent trying to keep up with the Jones'.

That's syncretism. That's dangerous.

BECAUSE ONE THING WE SEE IN SCRIPTURE—IF YOU HAVE ONE HAND CLUTCHING JESUS AND ANOTHER HAND CLUTCHING THE WORLD—GOD IN HIS GRACE WILL EITHER PRY YOUR HAND OFF THE WORLD AND IT WON'T BE PRETTY…. OR YOU WILL LET GO OF JESUS.

2. We Must Not Carry Disdain for Our Culture

This is what Separatism causes. Remember, the patriots of Jesus' day wanted their Messiah to lead them in a revolt against the pagan and worldly government of Rome. God did not bless their efforts—Rome always won.

And Jesus did not try to do it, anyway. It was not his mission. His mission was to change the human heart and make disciples. And that is the same mission the Church has been given— make disciples. With the moral compass of our nation shifting drastically, too many Christians have this attitude of, "I can't believe it! This is despicable! This country is too far gone!!"

That is not love for the culture; it's disdain.

And disdain for someone else, or a group of people, always stems from self-righteousness. Jesus came into a culture full of sinners and engaged with them. He entered into the homes of notable sinners, tax collectors and prostitutes. He let women with immoral reputations wash his feet. And by doing so, he ticked off the religious leaders, the Pharisees, the separate ones, who had disdain for the sinners around them and who were filled with self-righteousness.

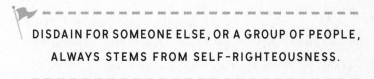

DISDAIN FOR SOMEONE ELSE, OR A GROUP OF PEOPLE, ALWAYS STEMS FROM SELF-RIGHTEOUSNESS.

And Jesus' response? He criticized them on a regular basis for their disdain of outsiders. He called them whitewashed tombs, "beautiful on the outside but filled on the inside with dead people's bones and all sorts of impurity" (Matthew 23:27).

Just because we said "Under God" and "In God we trust" and acknowledged our nation's Christian influence more in 1957 than we do now, doesn't mean we were more moral. The immorality was just a lot more hush-hush. Maybe we didn't see Ward Cleaver cheating on June on TV, but that doesn't mean moms and dads weren't cheating on each other in real life. It doesn't mean fathers weren't going home drunk and abusing their kids. It doesn't mean pedophilia wasn't happening at family gatherings and block parties.

Having Jesus' Spirit in us should give us greater compassion for the culture around us, not less. It should turn us into servants, not criticizers.

Because that's when people want to know your opinion. When we are known as those who serve the culture, who serve our co-workers, who serve our neighbors; when our churches seek to serve the cities we live in, when we stop keeping our distance by only going to Christian schools and Christian coffee shops and Christian recording studios, then people will start to ask questions.

If you're a public school teacher- your school should see what it looks like for Jesus to be a public school teacher.

If you're in finance—those you work with should see what it looks like for Jesus to work in finance.

If you're a business-owner—when people look at you, they should see what it looks like for Jesus to be a business-owner.

3. We Must Fight for Justice But Not Seek to Legislate Morality

This is a tough one to navigate and I don't pretend to know how to do it all the time.

But what we see in the Bible is that God commanded Israel to care for the foreigners among them, to care for the widows and the orphans, and to fight for justice.

When you read Church history what you see is that whenever the Church was marginalized and the minority, they just put their hands to the plow and did what they could for the victims of injustice. For example, because it was legal to discard unwanted babies, the Christians went out and picked up those little babies and adopted them as their own. As a result, they led the way in finally outlawing child abandonment and abortion in the Roman empire in 374 A.D. They outlawed the branding of criminals' faces in 315 A.D. They stopped human sacrifice among the Irish, the Prussians, the Lithuanians, the Aztecs and the Mayans. They granted property rights and other protections to women. They outlawed the burning alive of widows in India. And they led the way in abolishing slavery in Rome, Europe, Ireland, and then the United States.

We are commanded to fight against the injustices for those who can't fight for themselves. But we are not commanded to legislate morality, trying to get pagans to start acting like Christians. We don't see in any of their letters the apostles telling the Church to get those dirty Romans to stop cheating people or to stop going to bath houses. No, they were commanded to be honorable among the Gentiles, to let their good deeds shine. Actually, Paul said in 1 Corinthians 6 that it's not up to us Christians to judge the world. But it is up to us to judge those in the Church. In other words—those who are under the New Covenant in Jesus Christ are called to be holy and need to hold each other to that. But the rest of the world—including American culture—should be expected to be unholy and immoral.

So we need to stop acting as if only we would return to the Christian morals by which our nation was founded on, then we'd be okay.

John MacArthur, a leading evangelical pastor and theologian in America, who I disagree with on certain theological things, but who I agree with 100% on this one, said in an interview when asked how Christians are to view the rampant immorality in American Culture:

> *"The New Testament model of the pro-morality religious right was the Pharisees...Pharisees! They were the religious right, they were extreme. They were against everything that the religious right is against. They were for all of biblical morality to the nth degree and Jesus said, "Frankly, I'd rather hang around tax collectors, prostitutes and drunkards than those guys." Why? Because they had attained a level of self-righteousness whereas the other people, when Jesus confronted them with their sin, they broke under that and they repented and were saved. When Jesus confronted the Pharisees with their sin, they tried to kill Him."*

IN OTHER WORDS, THERE ARE MANY RIGHT-WING CONSERVATIVES WHO BELIEVE IN GOD, DON'T GET ABORTIONS, ARE FAITHFUL TO THEIR SPOUSES, AND ARE HEADING TO ETERNITY WITHOUT GOD!

Let's not confuse people by waving the morality banner in everyone's face, because we'll give the impression that morality is what Christianity is all about. It's just not. It's an imitation.

But it's not the real thing.

QUESTIONS FOR DISCUSSION

1. In what ways have you drifted into syncretism?

   _____

   _____

   _____

2. In what ways have you drifted into separatism? *Remember, it's possible to be guilty of both in different areas of our lives.*

   _____

   _____

   _____

3. How might Jesus want to live through you in a greater way in your current sphere of influence?

   _____

   _____

   _____

SAFE & EASY BELIEVISM

Back in the mid-80s, a commercial came out that I used to love to watch. It was for a little weird doll for kids called "My Buddy." I didn't own one. I didn't want to own one. I just liked the commercial because it had a catchy tune:

"My buddy, my buddy—wherever I go, he goes.

My buddy, my buddy! I'll teach him everything that I know.

My buddy and me—like to climb up a tree,

My buddy and me—we're the best friends you could be!!!

My buddy, my buddy, my buddy, my buddy—My buddy and me!"

And while the catchy tune played, I watched clips of the My Buddy doll riding around with little boys and girls on their scooters and tricycles, hanging out in the club-house, swinging on the swing together.

The message of the commercial was clear: get this doll, and he'll be the best of all best friends, because he'll do whatever you want him to do and he'll go wherever you want him to go. No arguments. No complaining. No putting up a fight.

Some of us believe in *My Buddy Jesus*. We said a prayer, asked him into our hearts, got baptized, became a member of the church, and now Jesus is our buddy. *Wherever I go, Jesus goes, too.*

It's the idea that Jesus can fit nicely into my current life. He won't shake it up too much. He won't rock the boat. He's cool sitting in the passenger seat. He just wants to come along for the ride. He just wants to tag along and see what we're up to, maybe cheer us on like our sweet Grandmas do. And when we want some space from *My Buddy Jesus,* we can just easily put him up on our shelf. *"I'll see you later Buddy Jesus! I need some time away from you."*

But that is not what it means to be a Christ-follower. It is a western idea—especially an American idea—that we can add Jesus on to our current life and call ourselves followers of Jesus. That we can make Jesus just a part of our overall life.

By the way—that prayer that most protestant churches in the West use to measure if someone becomes a Christian, that thing known as the Sinner's prayer, did you know that there are not too many instances where someone says a sinner's prayer in the Bible? How many times do you think someone says to someone else in the Bible: "Hey Simon, would you like to accept Jesus as your Savior? Just repeat after me..." Guess how many times that happened.

The actual amount is zero. Not once.

I had someone ask me once why I don't give people the opportunity after a sermon to say a prayer and become a Christian. "Don't people have to come forward and say the sinner's prayer to be saved? Don't you care about new people becoming Christians?"

So I asked him where he got that from, to show me in the Bible. "I don't know. I just see all the churches do it." Yeah, of course you have. You live in America.

Now there is nothing wrong with doing that whole sinner's prayer thing. Truth is, I do it from time to time after a sermon. But it's an example, I think, of how too often the gospel of Jesus is presented to someone, and then we say, "now just say a prayer and you're a Christian." Meanwhile, that person has no sincere desire to actually follow or know the real Jesus. They're told they will go to heaven and now Jesus will be with them wherever they go. Just like *My Buddy Jesus*.

But they're not often told things like this: *"Whoever wants to be my disciple must deny themselves and take up their cross daily and follow me"* (Luke 9:23).

NOW PEOPLE IN GENERAL JUST DON'T WANT TO HEAR ABOUT DENYING THEMSELVES. BUT ESPECIALLY IN AMERICA WE'RE TOLD WE *SHOULDN'T HAVE* TO DENY OURSELVES ANYTHING. JESUS SHOULD BE ALL ABOUT WHAT I'M ALL ABOUT.

If I like the Giants, he should make them win. If I'm a Republican, he must hate Democrats as much as I do.

And pastors and church leaders are largely to blame because we know people don't want to hear about the uncomfortable aspects of following Jesus, so we downplay them. It's hard to get those hands raised and people praying those prayers if we explain to them, "Before you raise your hand. Before you give your life to Jesus, you have to know up front—he's going to really change your life and flip it upside down."

It's much easier to just go, "Who wants a better life? Jesus will give it to you. Now repeat after me...."

EVEN THE DEMONS BELIEVE IN JESUS

There is a difference between believing something and having true faith. The apostle James said:

> *"You say you have faith, for you believe that there is one God. Good for you! Even the demons believe this, and they tremble in terror. 20 How foolish! Can't you see that faith without good deeds is useless?"* (James 2:19–20)

I love the sarcasm here. *You believe there is one God—Good for you! Congratulations!! Even demons believe that. Even demons believe the right things about God.* Faith without action, without a changed life, is just intellectual belief.

A friend of mine shared an analogy that I thought was awesome. Imagine there's a guy on a high-wire in a circus tent.

He's on a bicycle with a basket in front. Two guys are watching him from the ground. One man asks the other, "do you believe he can make it across?" The man answers, "yes, I do believe," to which the first man replies "then get in the basket." Getting in the basket requires faith. Faith leads to action. Faith leads to putting your entire weight into something.

I dated a few girls before getting married. And I believed in all of them. They were good girls. Good personalities. Good character. I believed in them but I couldn't quite get to the place where I put my faith in any of them as my wife. I could say, "I believe she'll make a good wife." But true faith would mean that I would get into the basket and ask them to marry me.

Then Jessica Thomas came along, and I knew—*I can put my faith in her!* So I did. And my life did indeed get flipped upside down in a good way.

JESUS DOESN'T JUST ASK US TO BELIEVE THE RIGHT THINGS ABOUT HIM, LIKE HE'S SOME COLLEGE EXAM TO GET AN A ON. HE WANTS US TO PUT OUR FULL WEIGHT INTO HIM.

In fact, when you read the gospels, you see this rhythm that Jesus had of building crowds with miracles and great inviting sermons, feeding multitudes—and then he'd say something offensive and thin the crowd out. Why did he do this? I believe it's because Jesus wants us to know when we're not really serious.

In America, up until the last couple of decades, it's been pretty easy to call yourself a Christian without much opposition. It all fits together nicely. But things are changing here.

Pew Research did a massive study in 2014 and published it in May of 2015. Using over 35,000 Americans, they found that the number of people who profess to be Christians has dropped from 78.4% in 2007 to 70.6% in 2014. That is pretty massive.

And you could look at that negatively, as if there are fewer Christians. But I don't think that's the case. Russell Moore, president of the Ethics and Religious Liberty Commission of the Southern Baptist Convention, says that this could be a good thing because it's an indicator that people who once were "pretend Christians" are now just being honest about their beliefs. He said in an interview with the LA Times, "Almost-Christianity not only isn't authentic; it's dangerous to people's souls."

I believe that God, in his love for us, wants us to know when we're pretending.

THE RICH MORAL RULER

Let's look at an example of Jesus exposing the heart in Mark 10:17–22:

> "And as he was setting out on his journey, a man ran up and knelt before him and asked him, 'Good Teacher, what must I do to inherit eternal life?' And Jesus said to him, 'Why do you call me good? No one is good except God alone.'"

Now we know from Luke and Matthew, who also told this story in their gospels, that this guy who ran up to Jesus is a ruler. A ruler means he was a man with power. And he was young. So this powerful, rich, young ruler runs up to Jesus, showing that there was some excitement there. He wanted to get to Jesus.

And he asked him what he has to do to get eternal life. *What do I need? What do I lack?* He knows that something is missing from his life. He maybe feels a lack of peace, a lack of joy, a lack of meaning. He wants eternal life, and although he may not know exactly who Jesus is, this guy at least is showing that he believes Jesus knows the key to eternal life.

Now look at Jesus' response. He responds by saying there is only one who is Good. In other words, "If I'm a teacher, I'm not good. If I'm God, then I am good. Why do you call me good? Do you really know who I am?"

But before the guy even answers Jesus, Jesus answers the man's question:

> *"You know the commandments: 'Do not murder, Do not commit adultery, Do not steal, Do not bear false witness, Do not defraud, Honor your father and mother.'" And he said to him, "Teacher, all these I have kept from my youth."*

So the guy is asking Jesus what else he needs to do, and Jesus refers to the ten commandments. But notice what Jesus does here—he picks all the commandments that deal with our horizontal relationships with others. The first four have to do with our vertical relationship to God, and the next six have to do with our horizontal relationships with others. And Jesus only refers to the ones that make us appear good to others. And the guy says, "I've been doing those since I was a teenager."

Now we also learn that this rich young powerful guy is also pretty moral. He follows all the commandments pretty well. Which is interesting, because apparently, if he ran up to Jesus, he must have sensed in his heart that being moral is not enough.

And Jesus, looking at him, loved him, and said to him, "You lack one thing: go, sell all that you have and give to the poor, and you will have treasure in heaven; and come, follow me." Disheartened by the saying, he went away sorrowful, for he had great possessions. (21–22)

Jesus looked at him with this love, this compassion, and then he said, "sell everything and give it to the poor."

How much did Jesus say to sell? *All.* That's a lot of time on eBay.

In the last chapter we saw that Jesus was not the right-wing conservative that we often see on the internet blogging about Caitlyn Jenner. But he's also not the liberal who thinks everyone should just give away their money and live on a commune together. It kind of looks like that here, but we have to let the whole Bible interpret itself. And we know that Jesus didn't do this regularly; he didn't go around telling everyone to sell all their stuff before following him. This was not part of the formula.

A formula would be too easy, anyway. That's how legalists work. Just give me the list and I'll follow it. *What do I do to show*

God I'm serious? I'll ace that thing. I'll go to church on Sunday, I'll sing a few songs, I'll read a chapter of the Bible a day, and then I'll sell my stuff. Legalism is just a religious version of the *My Buddy Jesus* mindset. I'll control Jesus by passing the test. That's how I keep him happy and pacify him.

So the person who says, "Yes, Jesus is my savior, but I'm gonna' do what I want in my sex life" is trying to maintain control of Jesus and keep him in a box. But so is the guy who goes, "I'm gonna do all the religious to-do's and make sure God thinks highly of me." Both are still trying to maintain control over this relationship. One is outright rebelling, the other is using religion and morality to do it.

That's what this rich young ruler was trying to do—*tell me what else I need to do. What else do I need to add to the list? Look at my spiritual portfolio and tell me what needs to be added to it. Do I need to diversify a bit more?*

> BUT JESUS, BEING GOD, LOOKED AT THIS MAN, AND IN LOVE CONFRONTED THE MAN WITH THE ONE THING THAT HE KNEW THIS MAN TRULY LACKED— SEEING JESUS FOR WHO HE REALLY WAS.

This man was looking for something to do, and Jesus gave that to him—sell all your stuff—and this man walked away sorrowful. Other versions say, "grieved" or "torn." He wanted Jesus, but not enough to part with his stuff.

And that's what Jesus was getting after: *You don't see the value in me. Your stuff is more valuable.*

FALSE-GOD-AHOLICS

Remember, Jesus told him about the commandments dealing with other people, and the guy said, I've got them covered. But the very first commandment is, "You shall have no other gods but me" (Exodus 20:3).

And what did Jesus just do? He confronted the man with his true god. He tells the guy, "You don't really want God. You want God to give you eternal life while you hang on to your true god, which is your stuff. But God will not have it."

It's not because God is jealous *of* other gods. He's jealous *for* us. He's jealous *for* you and me. Because he knows when we have other gods, our souls are essentially kidnapped by those gods—gods that cannot satisfy, cannot fulfill.

When you have a friend who is an alcoholic, what do you do? If you love him, you confront them, right? You point it out. "This is gonna destroy you, bro!" Well, we're all false-god-aholics. And Jesus is pointing out this man's false god for this man's sake.

And the man, instead of saying, "Okay I will, I'll do anything to follow you. I recognize you have the keys to true life…"—walks away grieved. Because he wanted something easier. He wanted something he could simply add on to his life. He did not think it would completely flip his life upside down.

But that's what happens when we truly surrender our lives to Jesus and let him be Lord of our lives—things get flipped upside down.

POOR RICH PEOPLE

It was common at that time to associate wealth with God's favor. If the guy has wealth, chances are it's because God really likes him. But Jesus flips that upside down:

> And Jesus looked around and said to his disciples, "How difficult it will be for those who have wealth to enter the kingdom of God!" And the disciples were amazed at his words. But Jesus said to them again, "Children, how difficult it is to enter the kingdom of God! It is easier for a camel to go through the eye of a needle than for a rich person to enter the kingdom of God."

He's saying the rich are at a disadvantage because they tend to fall in love with their wealth. They tend to be driven by the need to maintain their wealth, driven by the fear of losing their wealth.

And for those who live in America we are, by the world's standards, very wealthy. Even those of you struggling to pay your bills are wealthy by the world's standards. This is why the *My Buddy Jesus* nonsense is so easy to fall into in America. We love our stuff. We love our possessions. We love our trinkets and toys and hobbies and games and phones and homes and boats and cars and clothes and shoes and vacations. We love our stuff.

And Jesus is not saying it's bad to have that stuff. He's saying that when you own all this stuff, it's hard not to trust in it. It's hard not to treasure it. It's hard to surrender everything to Jesus as Lord when we have a lot of things that are important to us.

See, if Jesus just said, "You have to trust in me for the forgiveness of your sins," the guy probably would have said, "Cool, I'm in." But Jesus knew his heart would still be mastered by his stuff. And Jesus gets very practical and confronts him with the thing he treasured more than Jesus, the thing he believed in more than Jesus.

> HE SAYS TO THIS MAN AND TO US, WITH LOVE AND COMPASSION: "YOU MORAL, PUT-TOGETHER, WEALTHY PEOPLE WHO BELIEVE THE RIGHT THINGS ABOUT ME—IT'S HARD FOR YOU TO ENTER THE KINGDOM OF GOD."

And they were exceedingly astonished, and said to him, "Then who can be saved?" (v.26).

Who the heck can be saved? If the moral, successful people can't be, who can be? Jesus looked at them and said, *"With man it is impossible, but not with God. For all things are possible with God."* (v. 27).

The wealthier you are, the more you have, the more independent you feel, the more success you have by doing, doing, doing, then the less likely you are to fall to your knees and cry out to Jesus in desperation and confess, "I'm no good! I'm not moral enough or obedient enough! But you are good! You have paid for my sins! You are My Lord. You are my King. My Master. My life is yours!"

That's impossible from a human perspective.

But not with God. All things are possible with God.

When I was 18, I believed in Jesus. I knew the truths about him. But he was not my Lord. He was not my king. I had other things that were my gods—the dream of being a filmmaker, girls, friends, partying.

But God did not let me stay there. He did not let me go on claiming to be a Christian while treasuring other things more than him. In his grace he confronted my love for those things. And I broke. I was 19, and I finally hit a point where all my false gods stopped working. I bowed my knee and I said, "Okay, Jesus. You are My Lord. You are my master. Everything I've been chasing and treasuring—it's yours. Do what you want with it."

In the years to follow, he flipped my life completely upside down. And it was messy. Really messy. But now I can praise him for flipping my life upside down. Now I can thank him for not letting me just add him onto my life.

PUT *MY BUDDY* IN THE TRASH

I believe God may be confronting some of you as you read this. I believe He may be confronting some of you about the things that you are clutching to too tightly. The things you are treasuring too much.

For some of you, God may be looking to flip an area of your life upside down, and you're looking for an easier route.

Or maybe he's urging you to forgive someone that you don't want to forgive. Or to give away more money than you're comfortable with.

If that's you, I urge you to go with it. Surrender.

Say goodbye to safe and easy believism.

QUESTIONS FOR REFLECTION OR DISCUSSION

1. In what ways have you been tempted to treat Jesus like the *My Buddy* doll?

   _____

   _____

   _____

2. Is there something in your life that you are clinging too tightly to? That may have become a god?

   _____

   _____

   _____

THE HERO COMPLEX

I grew up watching movies like Indiana Jones, Die Hard, and Rambo (when my mom wasn't home, of course) and then I would go act out those movies with my little brother. And it wasn't hard for me to decide which character I would be. I was always the hero and my brother would be the bad guy.

Because every little boy wants to be the hero.

When I got my first crush on a girl in 3rd grade—a pretty damsel named Allison who had the hottest lunch box—I would fantasize about her. But my fantasies were not about kissing her or holding her hand; they were about saving her from danger. I would picture her walking down the school hallway, and then suddenly the chandelier on the ceiling began shaking and rattling (even though our school did not have chandeliers on the ceilings).

And with everyone scrambling to get out from underneath it, my damsel would trip and fall directly under the chandelier, right as its final screws came loose and it came falling down in slow motion. But, just in the nick of time, I would make it over to her and push her out of the way, only to have the chandelier crush me underneath.

Silence would fall on all the onlookers, as they wondered if I were alive or dead.

And then, finally, I would emerge from the rubble bloody and bruised, but alive. And Allison would run over to me and praise me as her hero.

These kinds of scenarios played in my head over and over again. Because every little boy wants to be the hero.

Little girls want to be the hero, too. But usually in a different way. They want to save the day by nurturing, by comforting, by having the right answers. I have three little girls—ages 5, 3, and 8 months— and the two older ones both already have a knack for putting their dolls to bed, nursing them, feeding them, protecting them.

And in one sense, being the hero is not a bad thing. Made in the image of God, we are designed to serve and sacrifice, and often times that leads to being the hero. The rescuer. The fixer.

> BUT WHEN WE'RE CHASING THE STATUS OF HERO INSTEAD OF SIMPLY LOOKING TO SERVE, WHEN WE PUT TOO MUCH FAITH IN OUR OWN STRENGTH, THAT'S WHEN THINGS GO AWRY.

That's when we're afraid to admit we don't know the answer to something. That's when we refuse to get help with our marriages. That's when we are too proud to ask for advice about our kid's bad behavior in school.

Let's look at two stories—one from the Old Testament and one from the New Testament—about our prideful desire to be the hero.

FIRST STORY: THE TOWER OF BABEL

In Genesis 1–2 we see the story of God creating the world and then putting humans in the middle of it all. He gave them a mission—be fruitful and multiply and fill the earth; spread out and fill the earth with image-bearers of God (Gen. 1:28).

But sin entered the world, everything was fractured, and within a short period of time we arrive at Genesis 11.

> *Now the whole world had one language and a common speech. As people moved eastward, they found a plain in Shinar and settled there.*
>
> *They said to each other, "Come, let's make bricks and bake them thoroughly." They used brick instead of stone, and tar for mortar. Then they said, "Come, let us build ourselves a city, with a tower that reaches to the heavens, so that we may make a name for ourselves; otherwise we will be scattered over the face of the whole earth."*   (Gen. 11:1–4)

God had told Adam and Eve to spread out and cultivate the Earth and fill it with God's image-bearers (expand God's kingdom for God's glory). But what are these guys trying to do?

They're trying to stay where they are and build a great city with a great tower to make a name for themselves (stay where they are and build their own kingdom for their own glory). They were resisting God's plan, and were fighting against it because they wanted to "make a name for ourselves."

They wanted to build a great city with a great tower so that instead of being scattered, people would look at them and say, "Wow, those guys on the plains of Shinar, they're something! They're strong! They're powerful! They did it! They came to this area with nothing and they built this great city! Wow!"

And this has always been a great temptation for man: *Build something great and make a name for myself. Use my strengths, show off my strengths, for my own glory. Be the hero that everyone talks about and is jealous of.*

This is especially tempting in America. Because it's the land where you can do that far easier than many other places. You can write a book, sell an invention, start a business, and be the next American Idol.

It's a great country in that respect, but it's greatness can also be our downfall when we chase greatness for the sake of our own name, when we put too much stock into our strengths and rely too much on our gifts, as if we are the Superman that the world needs.

But the Lord came down to see the city and the tower the people were building. The Lord said, "If as one people speaking the same language they have begun to do this, then nothing they plan to do will be impossible for them. (Gen. 11:5–6)

So God came down, in a sense, saw this, and said to himself (the Trinity), "We must stop this. If they do this, nothing will be impossible for them."

Now it may appear that God says this like an angry boss who's jealous of his employee's attempts to branch out and start his own business. But that's not the case. Scripture must interpret Scripture, and what we have is not an insecure God but a protective God.

When my middle daughter Sienna first started walking, she was overconfident. And she went for the stairs. And we had to realize, *if she can walk, she's going to go for all kinds of things. And not all of them are safe. She's going to put too much trust into her new-found strength at walking.* So we had to put up a gate near the stairs.

AND THAT'S WHAT GOD IS SAYING HERE — *IF THEY CAN BUILD A GREAT CITY FOR THEMSELVES, IF THEY CAN FEED THEIR EGOS LIKE THIS BECAUSE OF ONE LANGUAGE, THEN THEY WILL FIND MANY OTHER WAYS TO FEED THEIR EGOS, AND THAT IS EXTREMELY DANGEROUS FOR THEIR SOULS.*

One of my favorite shows is Breaking Bad. It's about a science teacher who is diagnosed with lung cancer and then teams up with a former student to sell Meth to make money for his family. And as time goes by, he gets better and better at it. Eventually, his wife finally finds out about his drug business, but he tells her that it's for the family. He claims that he is doing it so that when he dies, they will have money.

But his new-found gift of running a drug business soon goes to his head, and he is intoxicated by the power and the notoriety on the streets. In the last episode of the last season, there is a scene where he finally admits to his wife that he did it for himself. He did it because he was good at it. He wanted to build this empire for himself. And in the end, it destroyed him.

It's a wonderfully realistic picture of how much we can deceive ourselves. We work and work and work to build an empire for ourselves, while saying it's for the people we love. Husbands and fathers especially have been guilty of this. We get good at our jobs, and so we work long hours, more than we need to, say it's for our families and our kids and our spouses, but really we are building our own towers of Babel.

And losing our families.

Moms and dads can both treat their kids like little towers of Babel. We try to control and mold and shape our kids so that everyone around us would think, "Wow, they are such great parents. Look at how well-behaved their children are!"

Pastors deal with that temptation, too. It's extremely easy to say their ministry is for God and so other people would come to know Jesus, but there is always a temptation to try to build this empire for our own namesake instead of God's.

Come, let us go down and confuse their language so they will not understand each other." So the Lord scattered them from there over all the earth, and they stopped building the city. That is why it was called Babel—because there the Lord confused the language of the whole world. From there the LORD scattered them over the face of the whole earth. (v. 7–9)

So God, in his love for them, ruined their efforts to build a name for themselves. He took away their strength so that they could no longer build their empire. For those who belong to God and those whom he is forming into the image of Jesus— sometimes, in order to save our souls, he graciously and lovingly destroys our empires. With a compassionate heart that knows what is best for us, he sometimes takes away the crutch that we are leaning on.

So that we can lean only on him.

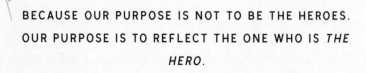

BECAUSE OUR PURPOSE IS NOT TO BE THE HEROES. OUR PURPOSE IS TO REFLECT THE ONE WHO IS *THE HERO*.

PASSAGE 2: PAUL'S THORN IN THE FLESH

In 2 Corinthians, the apostle Paul is writing to the church in the city of Corinth, a city that was, in some ways, a lot like America. It was a city where people could make a name for themselves through their gifts, where philosophers would compete with each other through their speaking abilities, where athletes could make a name for themselves through the contests, where rich people could erect buildings in their own names and at their own expense.

And so even in the church there was a spirit of competition. People would brag about who baptized them, they would chase after the gifts of the Spirit for their own glory, and false teachers would try to discredit Paul in order to steal the ministry spotlight.

One way that they would try to discredit him was by saying that all the hardships he faced proved that he was not a legitimate apostle. He was too banged up with too many struggles.

In other words, a proper apostle would walk in more strength.

And in 2 Corinthians 12, Paul begins to talk about the great visions that he received from God, but then he stops and essentially says, "I'm not going to boast about these impressive revelations." And he writes this:

Therefore, in order to keep me from becoming conceited, I was given a thorn in my flesh, a messenger of Satan, to torment me."

(2 Cor. 12:7)

Conceited. That means to be too focused on my own strengths, seeing myself as stronger than I really am, as the hero that everyone needed, as God's Most Valuable Player.

The word for "messenger" is "Angellos." Or Angel.

So in order to keep him from becoming conceited and too reliant on his own strengths, he was given a thorn in the flesh by an angel of Satan.

We don't know how exactly this demon was attacking him or what this thorn is. Some people have tried to say that Paul is talking about a speech impediment, which caused others to make fun of him or look down at him as a preacher; some think it was a specific temptation, like a bad temper or a sexual temptation. Others say he's referring to a physical ailment, like failing eyesight.

Whatever it was, it was tormenting Paul. The Greek word for "torment" means "to punch in the gut." It was a messenger of Satan that was punching him in the gut making him weaker than he wanted to be, less effective than he wanted to be.

Three times I pleaded with the Lord to take it away from me.

(12:8)

Now the phrase for three times was a figure of speech; he didn't just ask three times and then go, "Well, I've already used up my three asks. I'm done." No, it's a figure of speech that meant, "repeatedly, continuously." He pleaded with God repeatedly, as we should all do when we're suffering, as we all should do when we're getting beaten up by life.

But he said to me, "My grace is sufficient for you, for my power is made perfect in weakness." (12:9)

This thing was wearing him down. This thing was crippling him. This thorn was causing him to not be as effective as he thought he could have been in serving God.......and yet God said that his grace is sufficient. Enough. *"My grace is enough, so you do not have to feel strong. In fact, the crippling of your strength leads to a more clear manifestation of my power."*

Therefore, I will boast all the more gladly about my weaknesses, so that Christ's power may rest on me. That is why, for Christ's sake, I delight in weaknesses, in insults, in hardships, in persecutions, in difficulties. For when I am weak, then I am strong.

(12:9b–10)

God used Paul in people's lives in powerful ways. The Bible says that sick people would touch handkerchiefs that once belonged to Paul and be healed.

BUT APPARENTLY, PAUL WAS WEAK IN OTHER WAYS—AND GOD USED HIS WEAKNESS AS WELL TO SHOW OFF HIS POWER. TO MAKE PAUL MORE DEPENDENT ON HIM, AND TO SHOW THAT PAUL WAS JUST AN INSTRUMENT IN THE REAL HERO'S HANDS.

As a pastor—I face a lot of situations where I feel like I'm in way over my head, where I don't know what to say to people, how to help people. I recently pulled up to a house, about to go in to help a couple in their relationship, and I thought, "God, I have no idea how to help them. Just somehow do something over the course of our time together. Soften hearts, help them understand each other, because I don't have a clue what is needed here."

Well, two hours later, I was praising God for answering that prayer. And if he used me, I wasn't even aware of it because I was operating in weakness, in desperation, in deep dependence.

So while I should try to grow my gifts and skills, I also believe God will still put me in places of weakness.

To make me dependent.

On him.

So that he can be my great hero on a daily basis, in big moments and small moments.

FREE TO BE WEAK

How do you know when you're relying too much on what you perceive to be your strength? How do you know when you are placing too much trust in a talent, an accomplishment, a personality trait, a material possession, a career, your physical appearance, a position of authority?

One symptom is the fear of losing that source of strength. Do you regularly struggle often with anxiety and worry over losing that strength? Do you worry about losing that job? Do you get anxious about growing older and losing that smooth skin?

Do you manipulate conversations so that people know about your strength? Are you always finding a way to tell people about that game-winning touchdown you scored 25 years ago?

Do you get angry when others seem to be threatening your strength? When a co-worker gets promoted before you? When your younger sibling starts getting paid more than you?

Another symptom is the depression and discouragement that comes when you actually do lose that source of strength. When you find out your heart can't take another marathon. When you lose that dream job that everyone was so impressed by. When your perfect identity as a mom has just been crushed by a call from the principal's office.

Can you identify a way that you are relying too much on a false strength?

If so, and if you trust in Jesus, then read these sentences thoughtfully:

Because of JESUS, I'm free to fail.

Because of JESUS, I'm free to lose.

Because of JESUS, I'm free to say, "I don't know."

Because of JESUS, I'm free to walk in weakness.

Now read them again until they go from your head down into your heart.

QUESTIONS FOR REFLECTION OR DISCUSSION

1. Can you think of a time in life when you were confident that you were using your strengths for God's kingdom and his glory?

_____

_____

_____

2. What about a time when your strengths were more about your own kingdom and your own glory?

_____

_____

_____

3. How would you describe the difference between owning your strengths and becoming overly-confident in them?

_____

_____

_____

4. What is a thorn in the flesh that you are dealing with right now? What might God be showing you through it?

_____

_____

_____

DOMESTICATED GRACE

Do you own a pet? Maybe a dog or a cat? Maybe you're one of those strange animal-lovers who take delight in watching a snake slither around in his tank? Or a rodent walk on his wheel?

But how about a lion or a tiger? Do you have one of them roaming around your house?

Didn't think so.

Back in 1999, a woman from Jackson, NJ was caught with a bunch of tigers on her premises. She was caught when one of them got loose and ended up two miles away strutting through the neighborhood. A nice neighborly man wooed the tiger into his house, gave him some food, and called the Animal Shelter to come pick it up.

Actually the police came and shot the tiger.

Because that's what you do when a tiger is loose on the streets. A tiger is not a dog or a cat. It is not a domestic animal. You can't take in a lion or tiger and treat it like a house pet. If you do, it will get dangerous.

GRACE IN A CAGE

Many Christians in our culture have tried to do that with grace. We accept it—invite it in, so to speak—and then we try to domesticate it. We try to neuter it.

We buy into our culture's definition of grace:

Grace—the state of being agreeable, tolerant, and permissive;

MANY OF US LIKE THAT IDEA OF GRACE, BECAUSE WE CAN USE IT WHEN IT'S CONVENIENT FOR US, BUT WE CAN ALSO PUT IT BACK IN ITS CAGE WHEN WE DON'T WANT SOMEONE ELSE TO EXPERIENCE IT.

I don't admit it, and I'm not even always conscious of it, but if I was honest with myself I often see Jesus as a laid-back mild mannered gentleman who has mellowed out since the Old Testament. He is not so wild and unpredictable.

This version of grace leads to thinking that God winks at our sins; it leads to us judging others who are guilty of "worse sins" than us; it leads to us only believing some parts of the Bible while discarding the stuff that doesn't fit with our modern domesticated sensibilities (which our American forefather Thomas Jefferson did, by the way; he cut out all the miracles and resurrection stuff and made his own interpretation of the

Bible, without anything supernatural, because it didn't fit his modern Enlightened thinking).

And so here many of us are. We claim to be Christians who have trusted in the grace of God offered through Jesus, but we live like the tiger lady in Jackson—we think we can keep him tame, keep him around the house, no fear of him, no reverence for him.

And as a result, we do not experience all the joy and all the peace that we are meant to experience under God's grace.

FEAR OF GOD'S GRACE LEADS TO FREEDOM

We all tend to think that fear and grace are like opposites, but I think the Bible tells us otherwise. Let's take a look at a passage in Scripture that absolutely does not fit with any of our paradigms on life. It's a passage about an aggressive God. A wild God. An unpredictable God. But it's also a passage about grace.

And it's not in the Old Testament. It's actually in the New Testament. In the book of Acts. Jesus had just been resurrected, ascended into heaven, and the Holy Spirit has filled the first disciples. Peter preached a sermon where 3,000 people gave their lives to Jesus. And now there is a huge church. And then it says:

> And the congregation of those who believed were of one heart
> and soul; and not one of them claimed that anything belonging
> to him was his own, but all things were common property to
> them. And with great power the apostles were giving testimony

to the resurrection of the Lord Jesus, and abundant grace was
upon them all. (Acts 4:32–33)

That last sentence could be a summary statement for this paragraph: "Abundant grace was upon them all." What did grace look like? They were united, they shared everything, nothing they owned was 'Mine', they testified with great power about the Lord Jesus Christ. *That's* what abundant grace looked like. And Luke, who wrote this, keeps going with descriptions of what grace looked like:

For there was not a needy person among them, for all who
were owners of land or houses would sell them and bring the
proceeds of the sales and lay them at the apostles' feet, and they
would be distributed to each as any had need. (Acts 4:34–35)

That's what grace looked like. The grace of God birthed this unbelievable trust in God for their financial provision. So these early Christians were not only forgiven their sins, but God implanted in their hearts a spirit of generosity. Radical generosity.

Now Joseph, a Levite of Cyprian birth, who was also called
Barnabas by the apostles (which translated means Son of
Encouragement), *and who owned a tract of land, sold it and*
brought the money and laid it at the apostles' feet.

(*Acts 4:36–37*)

Then Luke mentions a specific guy named Joseph, also called Barnabas. Luke is introducing this guy because he will be mentioned in other parts of Acts. Barnabus is a man of integrity, with the gift of encouragement, a real servant. He was not the main guy, not a big-time leader like Peter and Paul, but a great supporter.

And here we see Barnabus selling a piece of land and taking the money and bringing it to the apostles saying, "Here, take this money and do with it as you see fit. Disperse it as you see fit. I trust you guys with this money. More importantly, I trust God. Whatever God can use this for to build his kingdom, I joyfully give it to him." He had this spirit of generosity because of God's abundant grace in his life.

Now before we move on—was this kind of generosity normal? Safe? Domestic? No, of course not. This was risky generosity. People don't do this. We might sell a broken lawn-mower on EBay and give half the money to God's work. But nothing like this. Where did that spirit of generosity come from? The grace of Jesus Christ. Barnabus didn't will it; it was a spiritual gift. God gave him the peace and the strength to be that generous. That's one picture of un-domesticated grace.

> But a man named Ananias, with his wife Sapphira, sold a piece
> of property, and kept back some of the price for himself, with
> his wife's full knowledge, and bringing a portion of it, he laid
> it at the apostles' feet. (Acts 5:1–2)

So here we meet another man, a guy named Ananias and his wife Sapphira, who sold a piece of property, took some of the money for themselves, and then brought some of the money to the apostles. At first glance, it seems like they're following Barnabas' lead. Maybe they're not as generous as Barnabas, but that's not a crime.

But Peter said, "Ananias, why has Satan filled your heart to lie to the Holy Spirit and to keep back some of the price of the land? While it remained unsold, did it not remain your own? And after it was sold, was it not under your control? Why is it that you have conceived this deed in your heart? You have not lied to men but to God." (Acts 5:3–4)

What's Peter talking about? Apparently Ananias brought some of the money from the sale and pretended that it was all of it. He pretended that he was doing what Barnabas had done. Apparently he came up to Peter and said, 'Here, we sold our piece of land, and although it was hard to part with it, we really want our church community to have the money from it. Here's what we sold it for."

And Peter, given a special knowledge or insight by the Holy Spirit, confronted him about it. And look how Ananias responded:

And as he heard these words, Ananias fell down and breathed his last; and great fear came over all who heard of it. The young men got up and covered him up, and after carrying him out, they buried him. (Acts 5:5–6)

That's how he responded to Peter's accusation. He died.

Now there elapsed an interval of about three hours, and his wife came in, not knowing what had happened. And Peter responded to her, "Tell me whether you sold the land for such and such a price?" And she said, "Yes, that was the price." (Acts 5:7–8)

So his wife comes in, and Peter confronts her, too:

"Did you really sell this piece of land for this price?"

"Oh yes, we sure did. That's all we got for it, sir."

Then Peter said to her, "Why is it that you have agreed together to put the Spirit of the Lord to the test? Behold, the feet of those who have buried your husband are at the door, and they will carry you out as well." (Acts 5:9)

I have no idea what Peter was thinking at this point. Was he angry at her? Sad for her? Scared for himself for being near her? But by this point, he has a strong impression that the same thing is going to happen to her.

And immediately she fell at his feet and breathed her last, and the young men came in and found her dead, and they carried her out and buried her beside her husband. (Acts 5:10)

I imagine the young men just finished burying Ananias and are talking about how crazy it was, debating about who is going to tell the dead man's wife, and then they walk in to find her lying there dead. "Why is everyone dying around here?!"

IS THIS NOT A PASSAGE IN THE BIBLE THAT WE KIND OF WISH WASN'T IN THERE? AREN'T WE TRYING TO EXPLAIN RIGHT NOW IN OUR HEADS WHY THIS SORT OF THING DOESN'T HAPPEN ANYMORE?

Maybe we're convincing ourselves that it was just a coincidence that they were killed, that maybe they just had a heart attack right at the same time as saying a lie. Or maybe their guilt gave them a heart-attack. It just doesn't fit with our domesticated sensibilities. I mean, sure they were lying, but that seems pretty darn severe. And it's even more confusing when you look at people in the Bible who did worse things than lie about how much they gave to the church. King David committed murder and God still blessed him big time.

It's confusing. It's not tied up with a neat little bow like we want it to be. This is a hard passage to read to our kids. I can just picture my conversation with my now-five-year-old daughter:

Kayla: But daddy, why did they die? Do we really die when we lie?

Me: "Well no....it's just that...um...."

We are not given a clear-cut explanation.

We are, however, given a clue in the last verse of this passage: *And great fear came over the whole church, and over all who heard of these things* (Acts 5:11).

Great fear.

Now you could argue that was just an effect of what happened, rather than the reason why God did it. But I believe God killing these guys was directly related to everyone else having a renewed fear (reverence, awe) of who God is.

POKING THE LION

Ananias and Sapphira's problem was not just lying. It was deeper than that. Let's look at some observations. This couple wanted two things:

1. The praise of people. They saw Barnabas sell his land and give all the money. They probably heard the church community talking about him and celebrating him and saying to each other, "Did you hear what he did! Wow!" And they probably wanted some of that attention. They wanted to make that kind of impact. They wanted that kind of reputation. They wanted people to say, "Did you hear about Ananias and Sapphira? Wow. What a great couple they are."

2. And they wanted their money. They didn't want to be as generous as Barnabus in order to get that reputation. They wanted the reputation without the cost. So they kept back some of the money and they lied.

   Peter said, "It was yours. It was fully in your control. You didn't have to give any of it and nobody would have thought less of you. This isn't socialism. It's your money to do what you want with it."

But Ananias and Sapphira wanted both those things, and they wanted them both more than they wanted to honor God. So much so that their strategy for getting both was to lie. *A simple little white lie,* they thought. *Doesn't really hurt anyone.*

But Peter said, "You have not lied to men, but to God." And then he added, "You have put the Spirit of the Lord to the test." What I think Peter meant here is that Ananias and Sapphira decided to lie because either:

1. They didn't believe that God knew they were lying. Which meant they did not have much respect for his sovereignty and omniscience.

2. Or they believed God knew they were lying, but just didn't think he cared that much; that because of his grace, their lying could be excused. Maybe they thought, "God will forgive us later for it. Not a big deal." These were Jews and they knew their Scriptures, and so maybe they even thought to themselves, "It's not like we're killing people like King David did." We're just telling a fib.

So they lied in the presence of the Holy Spirit, putting the Holy Spirit to the test.

THEY TRIED TO TREAT A LION LIKE HE WAS A COCKER-SPANIEL, AND THE LION FLEXED HIS MUSCLES.

Here was this church, receiving God's abundant grace, flourishing in that grace...and then there was this hypocrite couple who came in pretending—and God sent a message to the whole Church:

My Grace Can't Be Domesticated.

My Grace is Not Permissiveness.

My Grace Must Be Feared.

THE CROSS: A PICTURE OF POWERFUL GRACE

The Cross of Jesus Christ reminds us of what grace is. We needed forgiveness and we needed to be cleansed. We needed both. And because he is a holy God who cannot be near such un-holiness that you and I naturally walk in, justice had to be poured out. Jesus stepped up to the plate and took on that punishment, that justice, that wrath of God. So that you and I could avoid that wrath. So that we no longer have to fear punishment. At all. When we trust in Christ, we trust that he took our punishment. And now we don't ever have to worry about being struck down for our sins.

We also get his Spirit. Which changes us, leads us, transforms us.

We get both. Or we get none.

We can't reject his cleansing while accepting his forgiveness. To reject his Spirit's work in our lives is to reject grace entirely. If we think, "I want to be part of this, I like the idea of forgiveness," but then reject his transforming power and think that he winks at our selfishness and our rebellion—like Ananias and Sapphira did—shows that we never truly accepted God's grace in the first place. It shows that we're phony.

Imagine you're the eyewitness in a murder case. You are going to testify against a mob boss in an upcoming trial, and until then you are being protected by a police officer outside your house. There is always a police officer outside the door, risking his life to protect you from the murderers.

But now imagine that you, who are being protected by the police officer, think "Well, now that I've got a police officer outside...I can get away with cooking meth in my basement. The police are on my side."

That would be kind of crazy, right? If the police officer truly is protecting you from criminals, he will not wink his eye at your crimes. And if he is a corrupt cop who does wink his eyes at your crimes, he can't be trusted to protect you from the mob. All they have to do is give him enough money and he's going to go, "Alright, have him."

If we trust in the police officer to protect us from criminals, and he is willing to be outside our house risking his life for us, then we should naturally have a healthy reverence for him and we will not cook meth in our basement.

You can't use that police officer for your own selfish desires.

GRACE IS NOT PERMISSION TO SIN. GRACE IS THE FREEDOM TO CONFESS SIN AND THE POWER TO OVERCOME SIN.

If Ananias and Sapphire belonged to Jesus, if they had understood their desperate need for his grace—to both forgive them and to change them—you know what they would have done? I think they would have either given generously, or admitted that they're not that generous yet. "Here Peter—we wanted to give 100 grand from the sale of our land, but we're not there yet. We want to be there, but we're not there. So here's 20 grand."

That's what it looks like to have the Spirit of Jesus in us, to belong to him, to be set apart by him. We're free to just be honest about how far we have to go while simultaneously trusting that his power will change us.

FEAR LEADS TO FREEDOM

Let me close this chapter by summing up three ways that the fear of God's grace actually leads to freedom.

1. It Frees Us to Rest in the Protection of a Powerful God

We have a labrador at home—a cute little yellow lab named Sheila. She loves us so much. She loves us no matter what we do to her, how much my wife forgets to feed her, how much my kids kick her off the couch. No matter what, Sheila still has a lot of grace for my family.

The problem is, when I'm away, I don't feel that secure having Sheila protecting the family. If someone tried to break in, she'll run up to that guy with a toy in her mouth, wagging her tail.

But if I had a lion sitting outside my house, a lion that promised to love me and my family, I'd feel good about being away from my family.

Imagine that someone did try to break in, and my lion gobbled that guy up, and my security camera captured the whole thing so that I got to watch it later on. I'm pretty confident that my fear and reverence of that lion would increase, and I would feel even more secure having him guarding my house.

God striking down those imposters who were trying to sneak into his Church was God protecting his Church, his bride. And everyone else, who did have God's abundant grace flowing to them, had a renewed fear of it. And remember—that actually led to the Church exploding even more. Because they were reminded that God was still protecting them with his grace.

There is a book that was recently written called, "Fear God... or fear everything else." I do agree with the title. I either have a healthy fear of God, or I fear other things. I fear failure, I fear rejection, I fear loss of security, I fear discomfort. But when I think about my huge God, when I am reminded that God is a Huge Lion and that I belong to him, that I'm riding on his back, so to speak, then all those other fears become really small. My temptation to be afraid of failure, of loss, of people not liking me—they get so incredibly small.

And, of course, this passage reminds us that we can specifically trust God to expose the phonies that try to sneak into his church communities. We don't have to play detective. God will expose them.

We had one of these in our church a few years ago. He cheated on his wife, appeared remorseful, and wanted help rebuilding her trust. I talked to him about God's forgiveness of his sins. I talked to her about forgiveness. But within a couple of months, I found out that he had cheated on her multiple times and still was cheating on her. He came in on Sundays, listened to sermons, put Bible passages on Facebook, gave money, but was just playing a game.

And I had been fooled.

But God wasn't fooled.

Through many sources, God outed him. He was exposed for what he was—an imposter with a seared conscience. And eventually, after I found out about his lies, I said to him, "Bro, I know you're cheating on your wife. You confess it to her, or I'm telling her."

Why did I confront him like that?

Because I feared God FOR him. I was afraid for his soul because I knew that God cares so much about his children that he will go to drastic measures to protect them from phonies.

Unfortunately, this guy never came clean, and was even able to convince his wife that multiple women and the police department were all in a conspiracy against him, and they left the church.

He had no fear of God. Fear of God would have led to confession the first time this sin reared its ugly head. Fear of God would have led to humility and asking for help, even if he risked losing his family.

But at least God exposed him to our church and he's not around our women or children anymore.

2. It Frees Us To Trust in His Transformation of Us

Like you, I'm a work in progress. And this story, this demonstration of God's power, reminds me that just like he cut out of the church that which doesn't belong, he will cut out of me what doesn't belong. Paul tells us that

> *"he who began a good work in you will carry it on to completion until the day of Christ Jesus."* (Philippians 1:6)

HE WILL USE CONFLICTS IN MY LIFE TO GROW ME; HE WILL BRING TO THE SURFACE THAT WHICH NEEDS TO BE ADDRESSED; HE WILL BRING TO LIGHT PATTERNS OF THINKING THAT NEED TO BE CHANGED—ALL BECAUSE OF HIS POWERFUL GRACE.

When someone points out a weakness in me, if I don't have a big understanding of God's grace, I'll get defensive. But when I believe in God's big grace, I am free to say, *"Oh wait a second, this is God's grace on my life. I don't have to be defensive. I don't have to protect myself from negative criticism. God's grace is using this conflict to transform me and make me more like Jesus. I can trust this. I can lean into this."*

3. It Frees Us to Trust God to do the Impossible in Other People's Hearts

That guy I told you about earlier, who I confronted about cheating on his wife, was playing a dangerous game. And yet, God can still get hold of his heart. Because God's grace is not domesticated, it can still break into a hard heart like that.

As the early church was growing—around the same time as the story we just read—there was a young ruthless man terrorizing the church. He lobbied for the imprisonment and execution of Jesus-followers. He was a threat to God's people.

But God did not strike him down like many people probably prayed he would.

No, instead God got a hold of his heart and opened his eyes to the truth about Jesus. And then suddenly this man claimed to be a follower of Jesus.

As you would imagine, many Christians were like, "Yeah right. No way that guy can be saved. He's like an ISIS terrorist." But when this man came to Jerusalem, some others believed in the power of God's grace. Barnabus, the really generous fellow from Acts 4 who Ananias and Sapphira wanted to emulate, was one of those who stood up for this terrorist-turned-Christian. He basically vouched for him with the other apostles and said, "Guys, he's legit. I saw him preach. I heard his story. God has transformed him!" (9:26–27). Because Barnabas had a strong healthy fear of God's unpredictable, uncontrollable grace, he believed that this grace could break through the hardest of hearts.

And that terrorist-turned-Christian was welcomed into the church and went on to be the great apostle Paul, who would turn the Roman Empire upside down with his fearless spread of the gospel.

Is there someone in your life who you can't imagine ever turning to Christ? Someone who you can't imagine ever changing? Someone who you can't imagine ever giving their lives for God's kingdom? Perhaps God has given you a front-row seat to watch his powerful undomesticated grace break in and do something amazing.

In C.S. Lewis' "The Lion, the Witch and the Wardrobe," there is the famous exchange between Susan and Mr. Beaver as he described Aslan, the great King of Narnia:

"Aslan is a lion—the Lion, the great Lion."

"Ooh", said Susan. "I'd thought he was a man. Is he quite safe? I shall feel rather nervous about meeting a lion".

"Safe?" said Mr. Beaver . "Who said anything about safe? 'Course he isn't safe. But he's good. He's the King, I tell you."

> YOU CAN ACCEPT IT FOR ALL THAT IT IS, YOU CAN REJECT IT FOR ALL THAT IT IS, BUT ONE THING YOU CAN'T DO WITH GOD'S GRACE IS TAME IT, DOMESTICATE IT AND MAKE IT SAFE.

QUESTIONS FOR REFLECTION OR DISCUSSION

1. In what ways have you had a domesticated view of God's grace?

_____

_____

_____

2. Do you feel like God's response to Annanias and Sapphira's sin was too severe? Why or why not?

_____

_____

_____

3. Why is it important to fear God in order to find rest in Him?

_____

_____

_____

INDIVIDUALISM

Individualism? It's not wrong to be an individual. My teacher taught me that we're all like snowflakes—all unique and different.

Here is the definition from Webster's dictionary:

Individualism—*A belief in the primary importance of the individual and the virtue of self-reliance and personal independence.*

In anthropology, there is a scale known as the *Individualism vs. Collectivism*. Societies on the collectivism scale, such as Japan, ask, "What's best for us? How can we win? How can I improve *us*? How can I add to the corporation, the team, the family?"

Individualism asks, "What's best for me? How can *I* win? How can the corporation, the family benefit *me*?"

America, of course, would fall on the individualism side. Our culture says, "You have the right to go after your dreams, do what's best for you, follow your heart! Pursue happiness, and don't let anyone hold you back!"

And that's largely because of the Enlightenment.

The Enlightenment came upon us in the 17th and 18th centuries and it is credited for elevating human reason and individual rights. It pitted human reason against various forms of authority in society—like the Catholic Church and hereditary hierarchies. It emphasized individual rights, individual freedoms, and the autonomous self. Now, in one way this was very good because injustices abounded, the rich could treat the poor as property, and the Church abused their authority.

And in the midst of it, our nation was birthed—the result of Christian influence marrying Enlightenment influence.

In itself, still not a bad thing.

But because of our sin nature, we have taken the values of the Enlightenment and twisted them, perverted them.

It's what happens. If a society is not rooted in the gospel it will swing from the abuse of one set of values over to the abuse of another set of opposite values. For us, that is the abuse of individualism.

And many societal ills flow from it.

THINK ABOUT IT. IF SOCIETY IS BUILT ON INDIVIDUALS CHASING AFTER WHAT EACH OF THEM THINKS WILL MAKE THEM HAPPY, THEN OTHER PEOPLE, GROUPS, COMPANIES, TEAMS AND CHURCHES BECOME EITHER USEFUL TOOLS TO BENEFIT *ME* OR FRUSTRATING OBSTACLES IN THE WAY OF *MY* INDIVIDUAL RIGHTS.

So it shouldn't surprise us when decisions are made in the name of individual rights.

A recent Gallup poll found that 69% of Americans believe in euthanasia. I'm sure those 69% all have various qualifiers for why they are for it, but that's still a really high percentage of people who believe one's life is in his own hands.

Abortion is another example of this. I don't want to diminish the extreme hardships that young women find themselves in when they make the choice to terminate a pregnancy, but at its root is the belief that *my rights as an individual are more important than the life of this unborn baby. Only when being a mother fits with my individual desires should I have a baby.*

The extremely high divorce rate is another example of this. *I will marry whoever seems to fit my plan for me. When that person doesn't fit anymore, I will move on.*

Nobody thinks like that consciously, nobody puts that in their vows, but that's how our culture rolls. Remember the movie, "Titanic?" Rose was supposed to marry one guy that would benefit her family, but her heart wanted Leo. That was James Cameron tapping into what he knew about our culture. He knew we would all be screaming, "Follow your heart, Rose!! Go for Leo!" And, of course, her fiancé was made out to be a pompous jerk while Leo was an exciting adventuresome romantic.

But in first century Israel, people would see that as selfish: *Her family could be immensely blessed by marrying this rich man, but she's going for Leo? How could she be so selfish?*

We mock the cultures where parents arrange their children's marriages. But the truth is, we're not faring much better. Our individual desires lead us astray and fool us into thinking that: 1) *I know what makes me happy;* 2) *I deserve to have what makes me happy;* and 3) *If that thing that I thought would make me happy no longer makes me happy, I can discard it and shirk my responsibilities.*

This is a premise that, if we grew up in American culture, we bought into very early in life. It was fed to us.

And it's worse now than it's ever been.

When I was living in LA pursuing an acting career, for extra cash I would be an entertainer at kids' birthday parties. I'd dress up like Batman, Superman, Barney, Dora, whatever the parents called for. And I would entertain their little rug-rats—do magic tricks, make balloon animals, face painting, song & dance, that kind of thing.

And over time, I realized that my least favorite parties to do were for white people. Yes, I said white people. I'd go in there to do Tommy Smith's birthday, and halfway through the party Tommy's mom would pull me aside and be like, "Um, your costume is a little small. The head is a little bigger than it is on TV. You only did 5 songs, instead of all 7 songs that we wanted you to do."

And if, while doing magic tricks, Tommy came up and kicked me, Mommy or Daddy would blame me for his bad behavior: "Tommy is not happy with you. Can you please do a better job, Barney?"

It was horrible.

But my favorite parties to do were for Mexican kids. Because I would get to the party, and before doing anything, Grandma and Uncle and Aunty would greet me and go, "Barney! Come on in. Are you hungry? Take off your head, relax." And I'd eat with them for an hour, joke around, take some photos and then they'd pay me and I'd leave. Little Miguel would sometimes be off with his cousins playing hide & seek and wouldn't even get to see me.

At Miguel's house, it was a family party. But at Tommy's house, it was a shrine to Tommy, everyone bowing down to Tommy and making sure he's happy.

And guess who seemed to have more fun? The Miguels. 99.9% of the time. The Tommys always ended up crying in the corner for some reason, making Mom more anxious and Dad more embarrassed.

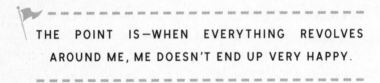

THE POINT IS—WHEN EVERYTHING REVOLVES AROUND ME, ME DOESN'T END UP VERY HAPPY.

HAVE IT YOUR WAY

For 50 years that was Burger King's tagline. You can have your food any way you want. Now I like to have my food my way. I like to go into a restaurant and say, "Hey, I see this chicken only comes with one side. I'd like to add another side to my chicken." I'm not complaining about that for restaurants. It's good business to tap into our Me-centered individualism.

But this has crept into the church as well. We Christians are guilty of elevating our individual rights, opinions, and desires to most important while disguising it with a cloak of false spirituality. We join a church (after leaving the last one because we didn't like the style of the worship music) and instead of coming into this new community asking, "How can I add to the whole?" we only wonder, "What can the whole give to me? What am I getting out of it? Does it make me feel good? Am I learning what I want to learn? Are they talking about the stuff that are my favorite doctrines? Are they singing the songs that I like to sing? If I volunteer, will I stand out in my gifts?"

We say, "I'm not called to do that" when we're just being lazy.

We say, "well, God told me" when we don't want anyone giving us advice about our personal lives.

We quit on relationships or responsibilities and claim "God wants me to be happy."

Paul warned Timothy about this in 2 Timothy 3:

But mark this: There will be terrible times in the last days. People will be lovers of themselves, lovers of money, boastful, proud, abusive, disobedient to their parents, ungrateful, unholy, without love, unforgiving...... (2 Timothy 3:1–3)

There is coming a day, Paul warned, when people in the church will be lovers of selves. And then he makes a list of all kinds of bad things.

We're so blinded by our self-focus that we can't see it. We even have Christians being taught that they need to focus on loving themselves more so that later on they can love others. It's the Bible filtered through the self-esteem movement: "If I learn to love myself more, then I can love others more because Jesus said to love others as I love myself...." I've heard some version of that more times than I can count.

And then we wonder why we end up like Tommy in the corner crying about not getting our way and moving on to another church.

THE GOOD NEWS TO MY ME-FOCUSED HEART

Jesus doesn't want us crying in the corner like Tommy. He is always after our joy. He is always after our freedom. And in Paul's letter to the Corinthians, we are reminded of his design for those who call him Savior.

Now it's important to remember that when it comes to all the churches that we read about in the New Testament—we read about them because they had some pretty major issues. Guys like Paul and Peter and John had to keep writing to these messy churches.

And one of the messiest, most divisive churches was the church at Corinth.

Not only were there divisions between Jews and Gentiles, but between the rich and poor as well. Some folks were getting drunk during the Lord's Supper. One guy was sleeping with his step-mom and everyone else was sort of winking at it, like "boys will be boys..." There was a spirit of competition and ego; people were bragging about who baptized them; they were suing each other; they were chasing the gifts of the Holy Spirit like trophies to add to their résumés. It was nuts.

Paul wrote multiple letters to them, two of which we have in our Bibles. Look at chapter 12 of 1 Corinthians:

Just as a human body, though one, has many parts, but all its many parts form one body, so it is with Christ. For we were all baptized by one Spirit so as to form one body—whether Jews or Gentiles, slave or free—and we were all given the one Spirit to drink. Even so the body is not made up of one part but of many. (1 Cor. 12:12–14)

Let me ask you something—how often do you consciously think about the difference between your hand and your foot? Most likely you don't, although there are many differences between them. You just use them for what you use them for. You're not thinking, *I sure wish I could turn door handles with my feet. I sure wish I could walk on my hands.* That would just be weird. Those body parts just do what they were designed to do, and you use them for different purposes, all of which are important.

Paul is saying in this passage that Christ's body is made up of all of us, Jews and Gentiles, slave and free, who have been baptized into Christ's body. We who trust in Jesus and have been given His Spirit have been grafted into his Body. Therefore, *I*—by myself—am not the body of Christ. I am *part* of it. *You* are part of it. And we have differences.

But when I'm functioning in this self-centered individualism that I'm prone to, then I'm thinking quite a bit about our differences. I'm mumbling to God about our differences. I'm frustrated with people who see life differently than me.

> ON THE OTHER HAND, WHEN I REMEMBER THAT JESUS OWNS THE BODY THAT I AM ONLY A PART OF, THEN I AM FREE TO CELEBRATE THE DIFFERENCES BETWEEN YOU AND ME. I AM FREE TO TRUST THAT JESUS KNOWS WHAT HE IS DOING WITH OUR DIFFERENCES.

THE ELEPHANT OF UNFAIRNESS

Paul goes on to acknowledge how unfair things can seem sometimes in community and in relationships with each other:

> *Now if the foot should say, "Because I am not a hand, I do not belong to the body," it would not for that reason stop being part of the body. And if the ear should say, "Because I am not an eye, I do not belong to the body," it would not for that reason stop being part of the body.* (1 Corinthians 12:15–16)

Let's face it—the hand is a little showier than the foot. It's a little more honorable, gets a little more attention. And the foot could easily think, "This isn't fair. He gets washed so much more than I get washed! He gets to wear a ring—all I get are blisters and callouses!"

Or take the eyes. The eyes tend to get noticed and stared at: "Your eyes are so beautiful!" But nobody says that about the ears: "I could stare into your deep dark ears all day long!"

And same with the body of Christ—some of us feel like we're just a foot or an ear. Not special. Not recognized as much as the others. We might feel a little insecure. Or we might get jealous of those who get more recognition, more honor. Or we may get lazy and think, *I'm not important here. I'm not singing or speaking, so they don't need me at the church gathering. I'm not leading the small group discussion, so they don't need me.*

But Paul is saying—every part is needed in each church community.

Do you get that? Do you get that the people in a local church community need you right now? Your gifts, your experiences, your love, your care?

> *If the whole body were an eye, where would the sense of hearing be? If the whole body were an ear, where would the sense of smell be? But in fact God has placed the parts in the body, every one of them, just as he wanted them to be. If they were all one part, where would the body be? As it is, there are many parts, but one body.* (1 Corinthians 12:17–20)

Think about a football team. Those who can run and pass and catch get more honor than those who can block and snap the ball. But are they any less a part of the team? If every player was a running back, there'd be no football team.

So Paul is challenging the whole mindset that says this church family thing is optional. *They don't really need me, so I'm just gonna' slip in, hear a sermon, grab a bagel, be friendly for about 5 minutes, and then get out quickly. Maybe I'll join a small group, so long as I don't get asked to be vulnerable. And if anyone annoys me, I'm out. I don't need any more drama in my life. I don't need a church to have a relationship with Jesus.*

But that's like if I, as a kid, said to my parents, "Mom, Dad—I really like you guys. I want to have a relationship with you guys. But I don't want to have a relationship with my two brothers. Can I work around that?" That wouldn't have been possible. We lived in the same house, and so we were forced to deal with each other, play with each other, fight with each other. I had to spend every Saturday at the Little League fields—and I didn't even play baseball!

When Cain killed his brother Abel back in Genesis, God came to him and said, "Hey Cain, where's your brother?" And Cain's infamous response: "I don't know. Am I my brother's keeper?" (Gen. 4:9).

Now the correct answer to that was—and is for the church— *Yes! He was his brother's keeper!* And the church, as God's redeemed people, is meant to reflect what Adam and Eve's family failed to reflect. We are our brothers' and sisters' keepers.

This American individualism which declares, "I'll answer to God for myself, and you can answer for yourself, and we're not gonna' get involved in each other's lives. I'm not gonna worry about you, don't worry about me"—it's just not biblical. If the foot needs scratching, what do you use to scratch it? Your hand. The hand doesn't get to go, "Not my problem. He's got the itch. I'm not getting involved in his itch."

The only way the hand would get that option is if it was amputated from the rest of the body.

But what happens to amputated body parts? They rot.

There's a lot of Christians out there, with a lot of head knowledge about the Bible, but who are keeping people at a distance. And as a result, they are rotting.

FREEDOM FROM MYSELF

Here's the truth that seems counter-intuitive to the way we were trained—when our hearts are rooted in this identity as part of the body of Christ instead of just individuals, it frees us. It frees us from the need to have things go according to MY plan, it frees us from the need to be the most valuable player in people's eyes, it frees us to do what Paul went on to declare:

> *If one part suffers, every part suffers with it; if one part is honored, every part rejoices with it.* (v. 26)

I played two sports in high school—football and wrestling. Football is, to me, the epitome of team sports. Every single play requires the team. Wrestling is more of an individual sport. As a football player, my priority was the team's win. If we lost, I was depressed. Sure, it would be a little comforting if I had a good game as a running back. But the team's loss was bigger.

Wrestling was different. How I did in my individual match was more important than the team's win. You could look up my individual record in the state's books. I loved that our team was good, but I was out there on my own most of the time.

Paul is saying church should be more like football. Even if you had a bad game, you could still rejoice when something awesome happened for the team. As a Pastor, I can make some bad calls for our church. And it's easy for me to be discouraged and be focused on my performance, how I'm doing as a pastor, how others think I'm doing as a pastor—instead of rejoicing in all the good that God is doing in our church.

BUT HOW?

How does one live in such a counter-cultural way? How does an individual like yourself, living in a culture that values hyper-individualism, live with other Christians like the true body of Christ? Like a football team? In an interdependent way?

Paul goes on in this chapter of 1 Corinthians 12 to describe different gifts that God gives to different people in the body of Christ. He reminds them—and us—that no one gift is more important than another. Sure, the guy who was used by God to heal someone may be talked about more than the one who simply cleaned up the dishes after a party, but they're both important.

And then he ends the chapter with this:

Now eagerly desire the greater gifts. And yet I will show you the most excellent way. (12:31)

Desire these gifts, he tells us. Go after them, pray for them. And yet—there's something to *really* desire, to *really* pursue. And now Paul goes into chapter 13, which wasn't a separate chapter in his original letter.

> *If I speak in the tongues of men and of angels, but have not love,*
> *I am a noisy gong or a clanging cymbal. And if I have prophetic*
> *powers, and understand all mysteries and all knowledge, and*
> *if I have all faith, so as to remove mountains, but have not love,*
> *I am nothing. If I give away all I have, and if I deliver up my*
> *body to be burned, but have not love, I gain nothing.* (13:1–3)

Our gifts are tools to help us love each other, not to stand out as the most valuable player. They are containers, dispensers of love. They are not meant to be the way that we gain glory and recognition and power for our individual selves. If my speaking abilities are for me, I am nothing. If I give up everything I possess to the poor, but it is done so that people go, "Wow, Chris is really giving"—then I gain nothing.

The word for love here is *agape*. There are four Greek words for love that Paul could have chosen from. The other three are:

1. Eros—which has to do with sexual love;

2. Storge—which was a parent and child, family type of love.

3. Philio—this is a brotherly affection kind of love, a love of partnership.

All three of those are good kinds of love, they are given to us by God and should be celebrated when we get to experience them. But it is possible to have those feelings of love and be self-centered.

The word for love that Paul uses here is *agape*—and this is a self-sacrificing, not-expecting-anything-in-return kind of love. It is the love of *me losing out on something so that you can win.*

IT IS ONLY THIS KIND OF LOVE THAT ENABLES US TO COMBAT OUR HYPER-INDIVIDUALISTIC TENDENCIES.

Paul continues:

Love is patient and kind; love does not envy or boast; it is not arrogant or rude. It does not insist on its own way; it is not irritable or resentful; it does not rejoice at wrongdoing, but rejoices with the truth. Love bears all things, believes all things, hopes all things, endures all things. Love never fails.

(1 Corinthians 13:4–8)

Is our love for each other patient? Are we patient with each other's weaknesses, blind spots, faults? Other versions say longsuffering instead of patience because that's what patience is—a willingness to suffer over time for someone else. A willingness to be kind to someone even when they are extremely annoying or consistently frustrating your plans.

It is not envious of each other's positions, jobs, spouses, kids, situations. It is happy when someone else gets the attention, promotion, blessing. It does not go, "But why not me?" That is a sign of self-centeredness. That is a sign of the individualistic *what's best-for-me?* mindset.

It does not boast. Boasting is not just the idea of outright bragging, though it can be. I've only been a pastor for 8 years, but I've seen people come into a church, get into a life group, small group, Bible study, appearing to want to be in community, but do it with the goal of showing off their Bible knowledge. That's boastful.

Often times being boastful and proud comes in the form of boasting to ourselves, in our own heads. It is when I meditate on how much I am doing compared to how much someone else is doing. Maybe in marriage it's meditating on how" I'm always the one taking out the trash." Or for church leaders it might be meditating on how "I'm the only one who really cares here."

Love is not proud or rude. Are you rude? Do you have to dominate every conversation? Do you always have to insert your two cents into every discussion because you think you're the most valuable member of your family / church / company?

WHEN SOMEONE INSISTS ON HIS OWN WAY, HE WILL BE IRRITABLE OFTEN BECAUSE OTHER PEOPLE HAVE THIS FUNNY WAY OF NOT DOING WHAT WE WANT THEM TO DO. AND EASILY-IRRITATED PEOPLE HAVE A TENDENCY TO BECOME RESENTFUL.

Which means they keep a record of another person's wrongs. They meditate on that list of wrongs. They recite it to themselves in the shower, they share that list with others—"she did it again"— and they carry grudges.

Notice again how Paul ends this passage:

it does not rejoice at wrongdoing, but rejoices with the truth. Love bears all things, believes all things, hopes all things, endures all things. Love never fails. (13:4–8)

Instead of assuming wrong motives, we believe the best about people. Don't miss the emphasis on *all* things. That's the main idea here. *Some* things, we get. I can bear with *some* things. I can believe that the difficult person in my life will grow in *some* things. But *all* things? That's not natural. That's not normal in this world. That's a different kind of love.

Jesus said at the Last Supper to his disciples, "Everyone will know that you are my disciples if you love one another" (John 13:34–35). Think about that. Our love for each other will be proof to the world that we belong to Jesus. Why will our love prove it? Because when the world sees Jews and Gentiles living in community with each other, rich and poor sacrificing for each other, extroverts and introverts being vulnerable with each other; when they see you and I being patient and kind to the difficult people in our lives—then the world knows there must be something different about us.

Then the world will know that Jesus really is alive—and he is alive inside of us!

QUESTIONS FOR REFLECTION AND DISCUSSION

1. What are some ways you have seen our culture elevate individual desires too high?

   _____

   _____

   _____

2. Can you think of a time when you have been jealous of the honor or praise someone else was getting because they were gifted differently than you?

   _____

   _____

   _____

3. Do you agree that being too focused on MY goals, MY desires, and MY dreams can steal our joy and make us more miserable? Why or why not?

   _____

   _____

   _____

ENTITLEMENT

Did you know that we all have an entitlement filter? It's a filter in our head that causes us to look at something and think, "I should have that. She shouldn't have that. I deserve it more. Based on my family background, education, experience, giftings— I should have what he has. Why does he have more of that than I do? That's not fair. That's not right."

We live in a country where we are entitled to have an entitlement filter. That was a premise of the founding of our nation: each individual has certain rights they can lay claim to. We have the right to life, liberty and the pursuit of happiness. The right to sue, the right to a trial, the right to free speech.

These are all rights that God has blessed us with, in this nation, when it comes to dealing with each other in society. This is largely because our forefathers acknowledged the *Imago Dei*—that we are made in the image of God. And as beings made in the image of God, we have certain rights that no other man can take away.

ENTITLEMENT WITHIN A SOCIETY, IN AND OF ITSELF, IS NOT A BAD THING. THE PROBLEM IS WHEN WE TRY TO TRANSFER THIS ENTITLEMENT FILTER INTO OUR RELATIONSHIP WITH GOD.

GOD OWES ME

We're all tempted to believe that our entitlement filters are accurate when we assess how God is treating us. We are all tempted to believe that, somehow, we have the ability to place God in our debt, that we can make him owe us, that we have rights that God must honor. *"God, I'm going to church, I'm reading my Bible—I honored my end of the bargain! Now what about you doing your part and answering this prayer of mine for a new job?"*

But when we read the Bible and actually absorb what it is saying one thing becomes clear, over and over again: when it comes to our rights before God, we have zero. No rights. No rights at all.

When it comes to my relationship with God, I do not have the right to life, liberty and the pursuit of happiness. Because if he gave me life, if I didn't work hard to be born, if he breathed life into my lungs, if he created my lungs, then my existence started as a gift. And if my existence started as a gift, then everything after my birth is also a gift.

So we cannot make God owe us. We cannot earn the right to claim anything. The Psalmist said, "Our God is in the heavens;

He does whatever He pleases" (Psalm 115:3).

Whatever he pleases.

I don't like that.

Imagine going to a doctor's office and there was a sign on the door that said, "Welcome. I do whatever I please." We would turn around and go somewhere else.

We would not want a phone company that had the disclaimer in their contract, "By the way, we here at Verizon reserve the right to do whatever we please."

So we certainly don't want a God who does whatever he pleases. We want a God whose arm can be twisted a bit. Who owes me certain things.

But that's just not the Bible.

Dutch theologian Abraham Kuyper said, "There is not a square inch in the whole domain of our human existence over which Christ, who is sovereign over all, does not cry: Mine!"

With my neighbor, I have been given certain rights under our government. If my neighbor accuses me of stealing something from him, I am entitled to due process from our government (although our government is also a gift from God, so is it really a right?). But with God, who is sovereign over all government and societies, I have no rights.

ENTITLEMENT ON STEROIDS

While this sense of entitlement has always been a struggle for humans, I submit to you that our current American culture struggles with this more than ever.

Our forefathers also acknowledged that with those rights come responsibility, a need for loyalty to our nation. As a result, we had individuals who were willing to fight for and sacrifice for and protect those rights for everyone. It was the idea that, *"I will lay down my pursuit of happiness to fight for your right to pursue happiness."*

Over time, however, our selfishness took MY individual rights and elevated them, while loosening our grip on the responsibility that comes with those individual rights.

This past summer I went to three funerals, all for men in their late 80s and above. And twice it was mentioned how that generation is known as the "Greatest Generation" (Tom Brokaw first coined that phrase in a book he wrote in 1998). It was the generation that lived through the Great Depression, fought in the 2nd World War and worked here on the home front to produce much material for the war. They were a civic generation, working hard for their nation and protecting the freedoms of future generations.

But over time, we have become more and more entitled. And you may be able to argue *why* that is the case, but you can't argue that it *is* the case. Personally I think it has to do with the assassination of JFK, the civil rights movement, the Vietnam War, the sexual revolution, the media exposing corruption, priests molesting children—all of which caused a growing distrust in and confusion over what we should actually be sacrificing for. So we've loosened our grip on our responsibility to society and say, *"I just need to look out for my own rights."*

But either way, here we are. A very entitled culture.

The Millennials, my generation, those born between 1981 and about 2000, are the most narcissistic and entitled generation of all. My generation doesn't know what it means to stick it out at a job you don't like because you have family responsibilities.

Technology has only served to make us less patient and more lazy. Need a cab? You don't even have to make a phone call. Your hand doesn't have to rise past your waist. You just reach in your pocket, pull out your iPhone, click on the Uber app, and bam. But God forbid that Uber driver is late—*oh, he's going to hear about it! How dare he show up late!*

Even with our shady behavior we've gotten more entitled. It used to be if you wanted to stalk a girl, you had to climb a tree, get binoculars, and take some risks. Now you can just stalk her on Facebook in the comfort of your own home without getting off the couch.

Self-help books and success coaches have all tapped into this and will talk about how you deserve more out of life, how you deserve a better outcome for your efforts—*and I can help you get it. Just sign up for my monthly coaching.* And they have us thinking, "Yeah, yeah, they're right. I do deserve more out of life. I've been through so much."

> ENTITLEMENT WITHIN OUR CULTURE HAS GOTTEN MORE AND MORE PERVERTED. AND CHRISTIANS ARE ESPECIALLY TEMPTED NOW, MORE THAN EVER, TO FEEL A SENSE OF ENTITLEMENT BEFORE GOD.

A MAJOR JOY-KILLER

Entitlement is incredibly dishonoring to God because it is the opposite of gratefulness to him.

And as a result, entitlement is a HUGE joy-stealer.

Nothing kills joy like entitlement.

Entitlement leads to:

- Anger at God when we don't get things we think we deserve. Anger is never fun.

- Self-pity. I don't know if you've noticed it, but thankful people don't feel sorry for themselves. It's physically, psychologically, spiritually impossible to feel thankful and also feel sorry for ourselves. We can be upset about something, but that's not self-pity. We can be sad and thankful, we can be grieving and thankful, we can be anxious and thankful, but we can't feel self-pity and feel thankful at the same time. Self-pity is temporary relief for a lack of joy, but it is not joy.

• Jealousy of others who are not working as hard as we are and are still getting blessed. Jealousy and joy cannot co-exist.

• Serving God in order to get ahead, which leaves us wondering if we're doing enough.

• Walking away from God because we're frustrated that he is not living up to our expectations.

But the problem is that we can't just decide not to be entitled. It is like cancer cells that are always trying to multiply and grow.

Look at one of my favorite parables in Matthew 20:1–16. Jesus says:

"For the kingdom of heaven is like......

The Kingdom of God, the way God's kingdom works, the culture of His kingdom—is like this:

"......a landowner who went out early in the morning to hire workers for his vineyard. He agreed to pay them a denarius for the day and sent them into his vineyard."   (20:1–2)

A Jewish work day was from 6am to 6pm. So a landowner goes out and grabs a few workers at 6am and offers them a denarius. Now a day laborer was toward the lower end of the socio-economic ladder. They lived day to day. A denarius was abnormally high for a day laborer. It's like picking someone up at

Home Depot and paying him 500 bucks for a day's work. More than fair. Generous.

> *"About nine in the morning he went out and saw others standing in the marketplace doing nothing. He told them, 'You also go and work in my vineyard, and I will pay you whatever is right.' So they went."* (20:3–5)

So then about three hours later he finds more guys and says, "Go work today, and I'll give you a fair wage." Notice he doesn't specify the amount. But they trust him and they go.

> *"He went out again about noon and about three in the afternoon and did the same thing. About five in the afternoon he went out and found still others standing around. He asked them, 'Why have you been standing here all day long doing nothing?' "Because no one has hired us,' they answered. "He said to them, 'You also go and work in my vineyard.'"*

So he keeps getting more workers and sends them to work in the vineyard. The last group arrive after 5pm—about one hour before quitting time.

> *"When evening came, the owner of the vineyard said to his foreman, 'Call the workers and pay them their wages, beginning with the last ones hired and going on to the first.'"*

Pay time. Starting with the last and ending with the first. This was not the normal order.

> *"The workers who were hired about five in the afternoon came and each received a denarius. So when those came who were*

hired first, they expected to receive more. But each one of them also received a denarius.

When they received it, they began to grumble against the landowner. 'These who were hired last worked only one hour,' they said, 'and you have made them equal to us who have borne the burden of the work and the heat of the day.'"

You see what this land-owner does? He pays the guys who arrived at 5pm a full day's wage. Then he gives everyone a full day's wage, ending with the ones who started at 6am. And the guys who came at 6am are like, "what is this? We worked 11 more hours than those guys, in the hot sun, and we got paid the same amount."

Did you ever feel like that with God? *What the heck, God? Did you see how hard I worked? Did you know what I've done for you? Way more than this guy? Way more than her!!!! Why does she get away with that? Why did you answer his prayer?*

And did you notice how in the parable the landowner made the 6am-ers wait to get paid last so that they would see how much the 5pm-ers would get paid? It's almost as if Jesus is teaching us that God might actually cause the entitlement in our hearts to come out of us. Charles Spurgeon once commented on this, "Possibly they first felt their vanity wounded by being paid after the others. They used their waiting time in considering their own superiority to the latecomers."

Does that ring true for you? It does for me. It feels sometimes as if God is *causing* me to feel entitled by making me wait for something that someone else didn't have to wait for. And it seems to me that Jesus is essentially saying through this parable, "Yes, the kingdom of God is like that sometimes." God is going to bring my entitlement out to the surface so he can deal with it.

He doesn't protect us from being a jealous, angry, whiny little child. He brings it out of us. He uses others to bring out our entitlement. Why?

BECAUSE WHEN EVERYTHING IS WORKING LIKE WE THINK IT SHOULD WORK, THEN IT'S EASY TO ACT GRATEFUL. WE MIGHT EVEN THINK WE ARE GRATEFUL. BUT WHEN SOMETHING SEEMS UNFAIR, THEN WE FIND OUT HOW GRATEFUL WE *REALLY* ARE.

MY PATHETIC HEART

When I was 18 years old, I moved to LA to pursue filmmaking (directing, writing and acting). Within a few months I became friends with a young married couple who were actors. Real actors. The kind who got paid to act. He even got the lead role in a popular Disney movie.

And I was jealous.

Because I had been directing my own home movies since I was 12, I went out to LA thinking, *Once they see some of my home movies, things are gonna get crazy!* But it didn't happen that fast. So I was a tiny bit jealous.

But he was cool and so we were friends and I worked through it. Eventually, I ended up going to their church, and then a few years later I got hired on staff at this church. And so I put my film career on the back-burner and jumped into this role with passion.

But guess who also got hired at the church the same week as me? That young actor friend.

So now here we were, both of us the new guys doing new things for this large mega church. And I felt a little competition stirring in my heart. I thought, *"Well, he may be a better actor than me. But I'm gonna stand out in the important stuff—the spiritual stuff!"*

And then his wife got a major recurring role on a popular TV show, and so they started making pretty decent money (which means A LOT of money!). As a result, my friend went to the church and said, "You know what—I don't need a salary. I'll still do all the work you hired me to do, but keep your money." And so now everyone on the team was like, "Wow, he's so awesome. What a heart!" And guess what little old me began thinking? *This is so unfair! I can't beat this guy at anything!*

It was pathetic.

I grumbled against God, and although I really really liked the guy, for a bit there was this jealousy thing that tainted how I interacted with him.

I wasn't grateful for my job, I wasn't grateful to have him as a friend, I wasn't grateful for him and his wife inviting me to the church that led to a changed life; no, I was jealous because I was guilty of entitlement.

And looking back, I think God specifically ordained for me to deal with that jealousy so that he could deal with my entitlement.

MY MONEY, MY GRACE

Let's get back to Jesus' parable and see how the land-owner responded to those who were hired first and were grumbling about how unfair things were:

> *"But he answered one of them, 'I am not being unfair to you, friend. Didn't you agree to work for a denarius? Take your pay and go. I want to give the one who was hired last the same as I gave you. Don't I have the right to do what I want with my own money? Or are you envious because I am generous?'"*

Notice what the landowner doesn't say. He doesn't say, "You guys are right. I can see how that feels unfair. I'll give you another denarius." No, he says, "You agreed to a denarius, and that seemed fair to you. Now it seems unfair? Are you angry that I am generous to others? This is my money. You do realize that I'm the one with the money, don't you?"

Another important thing to notice is that the landowner didn't explain why he did it. He simply said, "Take your pay and go."

Another symptom of our entitled hearts is that we at least feel like God owes us an explanation for why certain things are dished out and distributed as they are. *Why did you do it this way? Why do I struggle with my weight and she doesn't? Why do I have recurring infections and she was healed miraculously? If I can at least understand it, that would help.*

But the landowner doesn't even give him that. He just reminds them that it is his money to do with as he wishes.

THE SIMPLE POINT

Jesus then laid out a summary statement for this parable, which he didn't always do: *"So the last will be first, and the first will be last."*

Jesus is teaching that everyone who is called by God gets the same thing in the end, regardless of how hard we work now on Earth in this life. He's teaching that when we come under God's grace through Jesus, when we become part of the kingdom of God, we all receive equal amounts of grace, regardless of how much we work.

That's the point.

The work in the vineyard represents working for the kingdom of God on this Earth. Evening time is when eternity starts, the laborers are us believers in Jesus, the owner is God and the steward dishing out the reward is Jesus.

We will all receive the kingdom of God, we will all get salvation, we will all get God himself, we will all get to reign with Christ....

......but some of us will become Christians moments before we die, while others serve Jesus all their lives.

Some of us will suffer greatly for Jesus on this Earth, while others seem to be objects of blessing. Some of us seem to experience God's grace in the form of deliverance from trials......

while others experience his grace in the form of endurance through trials. Some of us will overcome temptation by God taking those desires away completely. Some of us will have to fight temptation daily. And it will not seem fair.

This parable is a perfect picture of how ridiculous grace feels to a system of "Work hard, get what I deserve," which is how religion works.

In religion we think we can control where we stand with God and how happy he is with us. *Screwed up this week? You can make it up over the weekend and re-balance the scales.*

But with grace, there is no control. No control over how God calls me, saves, transforms me, uses me in this world. No control. If I understand grace, I will be grateful to be called into his service, like those day laborers. I will be happy to do whatever work he gives me.

GRACE MEANS GOD REWARDS US ACCORDING TO
WHO HE IS, NOT ACCORDING TO WHO WE ARE.

FIX YOUR EYES

So how do we get free from entitlement? How do we resist the temptation to fall into entitlement?

The solution is simple.

It starts with identifying the problem.

The 6am workers were grateful for the deal…. until they saw what the 5pm workers were getting. They took their eyes off the land-owner, and put their eyes on other workers. That's when they started to grumble and complain and say it's not fair.

So the solution to entitlement is to keep our eyes on God and stop looking at other people and measuring how good God is to us based on other people's circumstances.

John 21 records a moment between Jesus, Peter and John on the beach after Jesus rose from the dead. Jesus has just reinstated Peter, and gives him the mission of caring for his sheep. But Jesus tells him that serving God in this life is going to lead to suffering for Peter and in the end death.

I would imagine Peter felt in his chest a sense of honor rise up within him: *Yes, I will die for you! Yes, I will do whatever it takes. I am your servant.* He's going to be Braveheart for Jesus!

But look what happens.

Peter turned and saw the disciple whom Jesus loved following them, the one who also had leaned back against him during the supper and had said, "Lord, who is it that is going to betray you?"   (John 21:20)

This is John writing about himself. So Peter and Jesus are having this moment, and then Peter turns and sees John following behind them.

When Peter saw him, he said to Jesus, "Lord, what about this man?"   (20:21)

Peter thinks, "Wait, is he gonna die, too? If he's gonna get to follow you and not suffer like me, that's not fair."

Jesus said to him, "If it is my will that he remain until I come, what is that to you? You follow me!" (21:22)

You keep your eyes on me. How I pour out my grace to others on this Earth is going to be different with each person. But you keep your eyes on me.

THE HIGH COST OF A FREE GIFT

In the life, death and resurrection of Jesus Christ, a payment was made. The wrath of God, which you and I deserve, was fully absorbed by Jesus. By trusting in his payment, we receive all that he paid for. We become adopted sons and daughters of the King of the Universe. We are forgiven for our sins. We become part of the Body of Christ. We are given the Spirit of Jesus inside us, which gives us the power over sin as well as joy and peace in the midst of troubles. And we are set apart for a future inheritance that will last for all eternity.

And since he accomplished it all for us, this means we deserve—are entitled to—absolutely none of it.

Zero.

The huge price was paid by Jesus.

QUESTIONS FOR REFLECTION AND DISCUSSION

1. Do you find yourself saying to God, "You are not fair to me!" about something? Where does that come from?

    _____

    _____

    _____

2. Do you struggle with self-pity? Are you often meditating on how hard your life is, always telling friends about the latest thing that has gone awry? Can you see how that is a symptom of entitlement?

    _____

    _____

    _____

3. What is something practical you can do to take your eyes off your "unfair circumstances," off those people you may be jealous of, and fix your eyes on the grace, goodness, and love of the One who paid it all so that you could have everything?

    _____

    _____

    _____

THE PROSPERITY AND POVERTY GOSPELS

In the 80s, Jim Baker was one of the top three most successful televangelists. His message could be summed up with his statement to reporters: "If we are to be fishers of men—that's what the Bible says, we are to be fishers of men—we've been using some pretty lousy bait. We've just built better bait to reach people." What was Jim referring to? The luxury cars, numerous vacation homes, theme park, and other "bait" that would show people believing in Jesus leads to luxury.

His wife Tammy explained it like this: "Just because I'm a Christian doesn't mean I don't like nice things, either. I love nice things, and Jim and I work very hard for nice things."

Their desire for "bait" and "nice things" went a little too far. On October 5th, 1989 Jim was found guilty on 24 counts of fraud and conspiracy. He was overselling life-time memberships of his new hotels.

But while in prison, Jim said he read the entire Bible for the first time, and wrote this:

> *"The more I studied the Bible, however, I had to admit that the prosperity message did not line up with the tenor of Scripture. My heart was crushed to think that I led so many people astray. I was appalled that I could have been so wrong, and I was deeply grateful that God had not struck me dead as a false prophet."*

THE GOSPEL OF PROSPERITY

America is the land where dreams can come true. The American Dream is, in essence, the idea that we can chase after and achieve the prosperity that we want. More than that—it's the land where we *should* chase our dreams, pursue wealth, and covet fame.

And it's no secret that Christians have spiritualized this American Dream pursuit: *God wants you to have it. All you have to do is trust in Jesus as your Savior and he'll help you get it!* The prosperity gospel says God wants everyone to be happy, healthy and wealthy RIGHT NOW. *Name it and claim it! Have some faith!*

But when the inevitable happens and we don't get those things, we generally have one of three responses: 1) God is not keeping his end of the bargain; 2) I do not have enough faith and am not praying enough; or 3) the people around me are not positive enough.

IN FACT, I WOULD ARGUE THAT EVEN IF YOU DO NOT BELIEVE THIS PROSPERITY GOSPEL ON AN INTELLECTUAL LEVEL, I THINK WE ALL BELIEVE IT ON A HEART LEVEL. I THINK WE ALL HAVE SOME DEGREE OF A FUNCTIONAL BELIEF IN THE PROSPERITY GOSPEL. HOW CAN I SAY THAT? BECAUSE WHEN MY PRAYERS DON'T GET ANSWERED THE WAY I WANT THEM TO, WHEN MY SICKNESSES ARE NOT HEALED AS FAST AS I ASK GOD TO HEAL THEM, THEN I TEND TO GET ANGRY AND IRRITABLE. THAT ANGER AND IRRITABILITY IS A SYMPTOM OF MY BELIEF THAT GOD *SHOULD* HAVE RESPONDED AS I ASKED HIM TO.

THE PENDULUM SWINGS TOO FAR

The poverty gospel is mainly a knee-jerk reaction to the prosperity gospel. This is where Christians respond by saying, *"No, no, no— God does not want us wealthy and healthy and happy. He just wants us holy. And the more we are struggling, the more trials we are facing, the easier it is to become holy. If you have too many good things going for you, then that means the devil doesn't care to attack you because you're not doing anything for God's kingdom."*

But both the prosperity and the poverty gospel are dangerous.

And both are dangerous not just because they are biblically wrong. Both are dangerous because they put our focus on stuff rather than Jesus; on our circumstances rather than on faithfulness to Jesus in the midst of those circumstances. And when our eyes are off Jesus, we lose our joy and our peace and our effectiveness in this culture.

FISHES AND LOAVES ARE GOOD

Let's look at a story in the gospel of John that takes place over a 24-hour period. The first part is very familiar and popular. The 2nd part—not so much.

> *Some time after this, Jesus crossed to the far shore of the Sea of Galilee* (that is, the Sea of Tiberias), *and a great crowd of people followed him because they saw the signs he had performed by healing the sick. Then Jesus went up on a mountainside and sat down with his disciples. The Jewish Passover Festival was near. When Jesus looked up and saw a great crowd coming toward him, he said to Philip, "Where shall we buy bread for these people to eat?" He asked this only to test him, for he already had in mind what he was going to do.* (John 6:1–6)

So you get it? Big crowd, and Jesus says to Philip, "What do we do about these hungry people? We gotta' get them some bread."

> *Philip answered him, "It would take more than half a year's wages to buy enough bread for each one to have a bite!" Another of his disciples, Andrew, Simon Peter's brother, spoke up, "Here is a boy with five small barley loaves and two small fish, but how far will they go among so many?"*

I imagine this was said with a bit of sarcasm. "Hey Jesus, we've got few barley loaves here. Wanna' try to feed this crowd with them?"

Jesus said, "Have the people sit down." There was plenty of grass in that place, and they sat down (about five thousand men were there). Jesus then took the loaves, gave thanks, and distributed to those who were seated as much as they wanted. He did the same with the fish.

When they had all had enough to eat, he said to his disciples, "Gather the pieces that are left over. Let nothing be wasted." So they gathered them and filled twelve baskets with the pieces of the five barley loaves left over by those who had eaten.

So Jesus did a miracle and multiplied the fish and loaves and all 5,000 people ate. We know from another gospel account that it was 5,000 men plus women and children (so probably close to 15,000 people were fed). And there was some left over!

In the 1st century, food was a big deal. You worked hard for your food. You didn't eat three meals a day. This meant you were hungry a lot of time, and so when you ate, it was a big deal. They did not take food for granted. And a full belly was rare. But that's what we have here—15,000 people with full bellies.

Have you ever been really hungry and went to one of those fancy restaurants that charge 30 bucks for a meal that ends up being the size of your thumb? And after you eat it, you're still hungry? On Valentine's Day in 2014, Jess and I went to one of those places, and on the way home we joked about stopping at McDonalds.

These guys had a real dinner here. By the hands of Jesus. Full bellies are a good thing. But then:

After the people saw the sign Jesus performed, they began to say, "Surely this is the Prophet who is to come into the world." Jesus, knowing that they intended to come and make him king by force, withdrew again to a mountain by himself.

It reminded them of what their ancestors experienced under Moses in the desert—manna from heaven. And they concluded that, because he was doing something similar to Moses, he must be the promised Prophet, the promised descendant of David, who would become a political king and lead the people of Israel into the glory days of freedom from Roman oppression.

So Jesus withdrew. Why did he withdraw? Because he did not come to be that kind of King. And he will not be that kind of king for us now. He will not be our money king. Or our comfort king. Or our luxury king. He will not be the kind of king whose strings can be pulled or who will satisfy our lifestyle desires.

OH, HE WILL BLESS US WITH PROVISION AND MATERIAL POSSESSIONS, FOR SURE. BUT IT WILL BE ON HIS TERMS, NOT OURS. IT WILL BE FOR HIS PURPOSES, NOT OURS.

MISSING THE SIGNS

After an eventful night out on the lake, the crowd found Jesus in the morning on the other side:

> When they found him on the other side of the lake, they asked him, "Rabbi, when did you get here?" Jesus answered, "Very truly I tell you, you are looking for me, not because you saw the signs I performed but because you ate the loaves and had your fill. Do not work for food that spoils, but for food that endures to eternal life, which the Son of Man will give you. For on him God the Father has placed his seal of approval."

They asked Jesus a question, and he doesn't answer them. Instead Jesus said, "You are not looking for me because you understand the signs, but because you got to have a good meal."

Now we have to ask, *what does that mean? Weren't the signs and the loaves the same thing?*

If we're going to Disneyland we don't stop at the Disneyland sign and camp out underneath it and then go home. No, we continue on towards what the sign points to. We may stop to take a photo under the sign and post it to Instagram as a way of expressing our excitement, but we do not stop there.

The physical food that Jesus provided for them was meant to stir their spiritual hunger for *him*. It was meant to give them a greater desire for that which the sign pointed to. But it did not. The people just wanted more miracles that gave them what they *really* wanted—full bellies, political freedom, a more comfortable lifestyle.

They just wanted more of that *which spoils.*

AND THAT'S THE PROBLEM WITH THE PROSPERITY GOSPEL. IT'S NOT THAT WE WANT BLESSINGS. THERE IS NOTHING WRONG WITH THAT. WHAT IS WRONG IS THAT THOSE BLESSINGS DO NOT STIR OUR SPIRITUAL HUNGER FOR JESUS, AND INSTEAD TEND TO ACTUALLY DULL OUR SPIRITUAL HUNGER.

The prosperity Gospel says that God's provision is the point. And as a result, we trust in our stuff, comforts, health; we cling to them, we're afraid to lose them—and yet at the end of the day our hope is in something that spoils. Those things simply do not last in this world.

But Jesus offers food that doesn't spoil.

Then they asked him, "What must we do to do the works God requires?" Jesus answered, "The work of God is this: to believe in the one he has sent."

What must we do to make God happy with us? Presumably, they want to do whatever will make God happy so that God will give them what they want—more full bellies. And Jesus says the work God requires is to believe in him. *Trust in me.*

So they asked him, "What sign then will you give that we may see it and believe you? What will you do? Our ancestors ate the

*manna in the wilderness; as it is written: 'He gave them bread
from heaven to eat.'"*

They're like, *"Okay give us more signs. Our ancestors ate daily
manna—can you give us daily miracles? We'll believe in you—but we
want to see some more signs. We'll follow you, but we want you to give
us the good life."*

*Jesus said to them, "Very truly I tell you, it is not Moses who has
given you the bread from heaven, but it is my Father who gives
you the true bread from heaven. For the bread of God is the
bread that comes down from heaven and gives life to the world."*

So again, Jesus is trying to help them look past the bread to
the giver of the bread, who is the true bread. *"My Father gave you
manna because the manna was a sign of the ultimate bread that he
offers the world—the bread that gives life to the world. Me!!"*

"Sir," they said, *"always give us this bread."*

Still, they don't get it. They don't get that the bread is standing
right in front of them. Their eyes are still on earthly stuff. They're
still focused on their physical needs and desires.

But that's our tendency when we face needs, isn't it? If you
need rent money, your eyes are focused on money. If you're
single, your eyes are focused on God giving you a spouse.

And the prosperity gospel capitalizes on that felt need and
promises if you have enough faith God will give you those things.
Just picture it. Envision it. See yourself with that man. See yourself

driving that car! But where's the focus? It's on earthly bread. Exactly the opposite of what Jesus is trying to do here.

> *Then Jesus declared, "I am the bread of life. Whoever comes to me will never go hungry, and whoever believes in me will never be thirsty. But as I told you, you have seen me and still you do not believe. All those the Father gives me will come to me, and whoever comes to me I will never drive away."*

I am the bread of life. I am the bread for the world. I am the bread that satisfies your ultimate hunger. Your ultimate thirst. And the Father is drawing people to me. Whoever comes to me will never be driven away.

EAT YOUR WHAT?

Let's skip down to verse 48:

> *"I am the bread of life. Your ancestors ate the manna in the wilderness, yet they died. But here is the bread that comes down from heaven, which anyone may eat and not die. I am the living bread that came down from heaven. Whoever eats this bread will live forever. This bread is my flesh, which I will give for the life of the world."*

Jesus says, "I AM the bread of life." I AM to his Jewish hearers would ring of God identifying himself to Moses as "I AM." There would be no mistaking it—Jesus is claiming to be the *Great I Am.*

But not only that—he goes on to say that we must eat him, which was a common metaphor in that day for taking something into our innermost being. Faith in Jesus means eating him, taking him in. Not just believing in him, but taking him in. Not just getting the right information about him, but taking him in. Not just reading our Bibles about him, not just listening to sermons about him, but taking him into our innermost beings. Seeing him as our true nourishment. Our ultimate need.

Throughout a given week, we all have felt needs— things we feel we need in the moment: *I need a coffee, I need a nap, I need more money, I need a new car, I need a new job, I need a new house, I need new neighbors.* Felt needs.

> BUT TOO OFTEN WE LET THOSE FELT NEEDS KEEP US FROM FEELING OUR TRUE NEED TO FEED ON JESUS EVERY DAY.

This past week I had a day where I felt needy for all kinds of things. But in God's grace he allowed me to face a couple of situations where I didn't even know what to pray for, and the result was that the biggest need I felt....was for him. I prayed, "Jesus, I don't even know what to ask for with these other situations, but I need to see you. I need to see *you*. I need to feel *you* right now."

And he was faithful to bring his presence and peace.

Because he is the True Bread.

But in this scene Jesus uses the word "flesh" which sort of throws them off. He will later give his life on the cross, which they didn't know, and his broken flesh would be the means by which he is the bread for the world. By trusting in his sacrifice on the cross, we enter the feast that is knowing Jesus.

But Jesus' audience didn't get that yet:

"Then the Jews began to argue sharply among themselves, 'How can this man give us his flesh to eat?'"   (v. 52)

They're still thinking temporally, materially, worldly. They're still thinking about this earth, this life.

And Jesus, being Jesus, doesn't really try to help them get it:

Jesus said to them, "Very truly I tell you, unless you eat the flesh of the Son of Man and drink his blood, you have no life in you."

Put yourself in the shoes of these Jewish guys, who depended on the high priest to make atonement for their sin each year through the blood of bulls and goats. For Jesus to say such a thing would be extremely hard to swallow: "Who is this guy claiming to be?"

Well, Jesus was claiming to be the ultimate sacrificial lamb, whose flesh nourishes our souls and whose blood cleanses us of our sins.

"Whoever eats my flesh and drinks my blood has eternal life, and I will raise them up at the last day. For my flesh is real food and my blood is real drink. Whoever eats my flesh and drinks my blood remains in me, and I in them."

Jesus is using quite a bit of repetition here because what he is saying is so huge.

> *"Just as the living Father sent me and I live because of the Father, so the one who feeds on me will live because of me. This is the bread that came down from heaven. Your ancestors ate manna and died, but whoever feeds on this bread will live forever."*

This life is going to end. The stuff of this life cannot satisfy in the long-run. Your nice house is nice, but it won't last. Your great job is great—praise God for it—but it won't last. You will be replaced by someone younger, stronger, and more energetic. Your health, if you have it now, will run out and you will breathe your last in this perishing body. But whoever partakes in the bread Jesus offers—*"the one who feeds on me will live"*—and experience true life forever..

WHOEVER DOES NOT FEED ON JESUS, WILL NOT HAVE TRUE LIFE. THEY ARE DEAD. RICH OR POOR, DOESN'T MATTER. STILL DEAD.

> *On hearing it, many of his disciples said, "This is a hard teaching. Who can accept it?"*

Only those who *want* to get it. Who are drawn in by the Father.

> *From this time many of his disciples turned back and no longer followed him.*

They saw the miracles, their bellies were full, but they left him. They turned around and left him. They didn't want to get what he said because they didn't want to partake *in him*. They wanted his stuff. They wanted his blessings. But not him.

I've seen this. I've seen people say, "I tried Jesus. It doesn't work. I thought I would get healed and I didn't. I thought my marriage would be fixed and it wasn't." And they walked away. But truly, they never knew him. Because they believed the gospel of prosperity, not the gospel of Jesus.

Like a used car salesman, the good news of prosperity does not come through on what it promises. And Jesus gets blamed for it.

But notice he didn't run after the departing crowd. He didn't yell, "Wait! I'll do another miracle!" He let them go. Then he turned to his closest disciples:

> *"You do not want to leave too, do you?" Jesus asked the Twelve. Simon Peter answered him, "Lord, to whom shall we go? You have the words of eternal life. We have come to believe and to know that you are the Holy One of God."*

We want you. Whatever that entails, we want you!

The apostle Paul later said, "I have learned to be content in any circumstances.... through Christ who gives me strength" (Phil. 4:11, 13). *Christ is my source of life no matter what. When I'm rich, I don't trust in my riches for life. When I'm poor, I am still rich with Jesus!*

Now don't forget—Jesus did the miracle. He provided the fish and loaves. But he did it to point to him. So don't swing the other way of *I'm not gonna ask for anything, God doesn't want to bless me with a better-paying job, God doesn't want to heal me.* Don't go there! Pray, pursue miracles, believe for them. But when you are blessed, let those blessings point you past the blessings to the giver of the blessings.

I prayed for a wife for a long time. Jess was the answer to those prayers. But guess what—she is not the bread of life. She does not bring me unending satisfaction. She does not offer me eternal life. As great as it is being married to Jess, Jesus is that much better. And one day, I will get all the prosperity that he purchased for me.

If you have a great job, if you're making a lot of money—be faithful with that money. If you can make more money, make more money! But be faithful. Remember it's Jesus' money.

If you're sick, pray for healing. Ask others to pray over for you for healing. Expect it. But at the same time, realize that one day every sickness will be completely eradicated by Jesus and you will get a new body.

IN THE MEANTIME

While you're waiting for that miracle, that healing, that blessing, that provision—in the meantime, there is one proper response.

Before you try to figure out what you need to do to change things—if you should apply to a different job, if you should go to a different doctor—before all those things, there is one proper response:

> *Though the fig tree does not bud*
> *and there are no grapes on the vines,*
> *though the olive crop fails*
> *and the fields produce no food,*
> *though there are no sheep in the pen*
> *and no cattle in the stalls.....*
> *yet I will rejoice in the Lord,*
> *I will be joyful in God my Savior.*
> *The Sovereign Lord is my strength;*
> *he makes my feet like the feet of a deer,*
> *he enables me to tread on the heights*   (Habakkuk 3:17–19)

That is the response when he is our ultimate bread. We will rejoice in him. We rejoice that we can have *him*, even when everything else is falling apart. When we trust in Jesus as Savior, the true bread whose flesh was broken so that we could be made whole, we can continually feed spiritually on him in all circumstances.

QUESTIONS FOR REFLECTION AND DISCUSSION

1. Are you more prone to give into the prosperity gospel or the poverty gospel? And why?

    _____

    _____

    _____

2. In what ways can you practically rejoice in Jesus as your true bread through the blessings in your life?

_____

_____

_____

3. In what ways can you practically rejoice in Jesus as your true bread through the difficulties in your life?

_____

_____

_____

BUSY BUT LAZY

I've never heard a parent brag, "I'm really proud of my teenage son—he's so lazy." I've never heard a young single woman say, "I'm not very picky. I just want a man who is handsome, loves kids, and doesn't like to work."

No, nobody claims laziness as a virtue. We have different lines for when laziness becomes laziness, but nobody would argue that laziness is a good thing.

I bet you would not identify yourself as lazy. After all, you're reading a book. Who reads books anymore, with our short attention spans? Only the non-lazy, of course. And that's you!

No, you're not lazy. You may even be reading this book while working out on an exercise bike at the gym. In between taking calls from your co-workers who can't seem to figure out how to get anything done without your help.

Or maybe you're reading while your laundry is drying and your kids are lying down for their one nap of the day that only seems to last 10 minutes.

You are not lazy.

Because you're an American. And America is a busy society. In this country we live lives full of unending activity.

And it's only getting busier and busier.

When I was a kid, you could only do one or two activities every season. Now there are 56 sports each season; you can play baseball and basketball all year round; and there are All-star leagues for the all-star teams.

Our phones and iPads make it so that we are always engaged in something. If there's a line at the post office, I can respond to a few emails. If my wife goes to the bathroom while we're at a restaurant, I can quickly "like" a few of my friends' posts on Facebook. If I get bored at my daughter's recital, I can read a recent NY Times article.

We are a busy society and that means we can't be lazy.

Or so they say.

THE POINT OF DIMINISHING RETURNS

Is it possible to be so busy that we become distracted from the important things….and thus become lazy about those important things?

I think it's more than possible; it's our tendency.

It's *my* tendency.

Both my wife and I would say that our marriage is more important than our jobs. And yet, we can easily take advantage of a few moments of silence at the end of the day by jumping on our laptops to get ahead on work projects—only to miss the opportunity to connect with each other.

I can miss opportunities to get to know other guys at the gym because I'm listening to a podcast.

My days off can get so filled with errands and social stuff that I don't take the time to rest in God's presence.

AND WHAT HAPPENS IS THAT MY HEART CAN BE SO PREOCCUPIED WITH STUFF THAT IT ACTUALLY BECOMES DULL AND COMPLACENT TOWARDS THE THINGS THAT I SHOULD BE FIRED UP AND PASSIONATE ABOUT.

And I think that is the case for a lot of us in our culture.

THE PHOTO THAT WOKE AMERICA UP

Do you know who Bill Hudson was? If you're my age or younger, probably not. I didn't until recently. He was a photojournalist for the Associated Press, who, at the age of 29, took a photograph in 1963 of a German-Shepherd police dog attacking a black high school boy.

The next day that photograph took up three columns in the New York Times, and it is argued that this photograph played a major role to drive international opinion to side with the civil rights movement.

Why did it take a photograph?

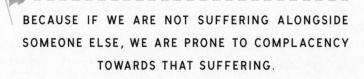

BECAUSE IF WE ARE NOT SUFFERING ALONGSIDE SOMEONE ELSE, WE ARE PRONE TO COMPLACENCY TOWARDS THAT SUFFERING.

We are prone to be wrapped up in our own little worlds. We are prone, especially in our culture, to live as if this is peace-time—as if the battles are going on over in Syria and Iraq—when the Bible paints the picture that we are always, as long as we are alive on this earth, in a spiritual battle.

God is on a mission to make disciples, to take people who naturally don't love him and love ourselves more than anything else, and to rescue our hearts and reshape them so that we worship him above all things and are used by him to rescue others. That's God's mission.

But Satan is on a mission, too. Satan is on a mission to steal our worship, to take our eyes off of how great God is and cause us to focus on ourselves and our own kingdoms and to forget what God is doing.

And Satan has many tactics. Satan comes after us in many ways.

CHOKED OUT BY GOOD STUFF

One of Jesus' most famous parables tells of his various tactics:

> And he was teaching them many things in parables, and in his teaching he said to them: "Listen! Behold, a sower went out to sow.

> And as he sowed, some seed fell along the path, and the birds came and devoured it. Other seed fell on rocky ground, where it did not have much soil, and immediately it sprang up, since it had no depth of soil. And when the sun rose, it was scorched, and since it had no root, it withered away.

> Other seed fell among thorns, and the thorns grew up and choked it, and it yielded no grain. And other seeds fell into good soil and produced grain, growing up and increasing and yielding thirtyfold and sixtyfold and a hundredfold." And he said, "He who has ears to hear, let him hear."   (Mark 4:2–9)

So that's the parable. No explanation. *Whoever has ears to hear, listen up.* The next three verses are about how the 12 disciples came to Jesus later, after the crowd left, and asked, "Why are you always talking in parables? They're confusing." And Jesus' answer is pretty much, "So that people who don't want to understand won't understand." *Uh.... okay.*

But then he explains it in verses 13–20:

And he said to them, "Do you not understand this parable? How then will you understand all the parables? The farmer sows the word. (Mark 4:13–14)

The seed is the Word—the good news that Jesus brings. Jesus is the farmer doing to the crowds what he talks about in this parable—sowing the word that brings life, the word that brings freedom, joy, peace.

And these are the ones along the path, where the word is sown: when they hear, Satan immediately comes and takes away the word that is sown in them. (4:15)

Some people hear the good news, they hear the message of Jesus Christ, and quickly it goes in one ear and out the other. It happened with many in the crowds that were listening to Jesus. It may happen to some of you right now as you are reading.

And these are the ones sown on rocky ground: the ones who, when they hear the word, immediately receive it with joy. And they have no root in themselves, but endure for a while; then, when tribulation or persecution arises on account of the word, immediately they fall away." (4:16–17)

The second group are those whose hearts are like rocky soil. The seeds go in and they receive the good news of Jesus with joy—and that appears to be awesome. They're excited. But when trouble and persecution come they say, "Forget this, I can't do that. I can't obey God in this area. I can't keep following Jesus if it means I sacrifice this. I can't put up with the persecution, the threats, the danger that it brings. The loss of fun, the criticism from friends."

But the next kind of soil is what we're focusing on in this chapter.

"And others are the ones sown among thorns. They are those who hear the word, but the cares of the world and the deceitfulness of riches and the desires for other things enter in and choke the word, and it proves unfruitful.

Others, like seed sown on good soil, hear the word, accept it, and produce a crop—some thirty, some sixty, some a hundred times what was sown." (4:18–20)

Thorns and weeds grow and choke out the word, the good news of God's grace. What are the thorns? They are the cares of life, the deceitfulness of wealth and the desires for other things. They choke out the word, making it unfruitful.

And it's contrasted with the good soil, which did bear fruit—30,60, and 100-fold, exponential fruit-bearing.

This fruit-bearing refers to, I believe, us as individuals growing and becoming more like Jesus, and *also* making disciples of others and helping them grow.

If I was to come up with a phrase to summarize what it means to be fruitful, I would say: "Being the good news of Jesus to this world full of bad news." But all too often, we are prevented by it because of the thorns that we allow in. By the cares of this world.

DISTRACTIONS DISGUISED AS CARES

When I go to the mall I am on a mission to get my phone or computer fixed and get out as quickly as possible (because those are the only reasons I really go to the mall). In the process, I walk by dozens and dozens of human beings and look at them like they are apparel.

I don't naturally walk by them and think, *That person matters to God. That person is made in the image of God and matters to God.'* Why? Because I'm annoyed that I broke another phone and just want to get it fixed and get on with my day.

The Greek word for cares, as used in Jesus' parable, is *mer'-im-nah.* It comes from the root word *merizo,* which means distraction, something that divides. The distractions of the current age. Being distracted by the preoccupations of the current age. And these pre-occupations choke out what Jesus is trying to do in us and through us for the sake of others and for his kingdom.

THE DECEITFULNESS OF RICHES

This is about believing that wealth makes us safe; being deceived by our wealth into thinking that this world is our home.

When we first moved to Brick, the town we currently live in on the Jersey Shore, I would walk around our neighborhood praying for my neighbors and praying for the mission of True Life Church in Brick.

Three years later, I don't do that as much. Why? Because this has become home. We have a nice house, a nice yard, routines established, there are rhythms we've fallen into with neighbors (like the same conversations over and over with them) and so I've become comfortable. I have been lulled to sleep. We are not wealthy by America's standards, but we certainly are by the world's standards. And that wealth has lulled me to sleep.

> **LIVING IN AMERICA CAN BE SO DECEIVING BECAUSE IT FEELS LIKE PEACETIME. WE FORGET THAT THERE IS A SPIRITUAL BATTLE GOING ON. AND WHEN WE THINK WE'RE AT PEACE TIME, THEN WE GET SELFISH AND WE FOCUS ON OUR OWN LITTLE KINGDOMS.**

2014 saw the worst outbreaks of Ebola in human history, killing between 5,000 and 15,000 (they use statistical models to estimate as they can't be sure). But let's face it—we didn't really care about it until the first American died, until it hit American soil. Then we finally woke up to it. Because when we feel separate, safe, then we're prone to be complacent towards the brokenness and hurts of the world around us.

DESIRES FOR OTHER THINGS

Jesus also said that the thorns represent our desires for other things. What kind of things? Things that are not fruit. Things that don't count for eternity. Things that have no value in God's eyes.

Apple knows that we always want more stuff, so they come out with a new iPhone every other month. And we fall for it. We take the time to upgrade constantly.

We always want more. We want more comforts, we want more accolades, we want more attention, we want more praise, we want what we think we're entitled to. We get so preoccupied with what the rest of the culture chases after it's as if—we don't consciously say it, of course—our mission is *ME and my family.*

FROZEN

Towards of the end of the movie *Saving Private Ryan* there is an intense and brutal knife fight between an American soldier and a Nazi soldier. They are clawing and pounding on each other, knowing that only one of them is going to live through this.

Just a few feet away, with a loaded rifle, is a fellow American soldier. He has the power and the opportunity to end this fight, to take out the Nazi, to save his comrade.

The fight comes to a climax, with the German on top and in control of the knife, which is just inches away from the heart of the American. With the weight of his body bearing down on the knife, it's only a matter of seconds before it enters the American's chest.

What a moment it would have been if at the last second a shot rings out and the German fell over dead—killed by the hero who came to his buddy's rescue.

But that's not what happened. Instead, the man with the gun, the comrade who had the power to take out the Nazi, the American soldier who could have saved his friend—he froze.

He froze in passivity. As a result, his partner died.

Because he didn't do what he was called to do.

AND THAT'S WHAT HAPPENS WHEN WE ARE CHOKED AND STRANGLED BY THE CARES OF THE WORLD AND THE DECEITFULNESS OF WEALTH—WE DON'T DO WHAT WE ARE CALLED TO DO, WHICH IS TO BEAR FRUIT.

To make disciples. And demonstrate—at the cost of our own desires—the love of Jesus to the world.

ISIS has slaughtered thousands and thousands of Christians and Muslims around the world, primarily in the Middle East. There are between 50 and 200 thousand new orphans (they don't know for sure because these orphans are on the run and in war zones so they're not being tagged or registered in orphanages). I'll admit that for myself, up until recently, it felt like something happening *over there*. Until I heard about a little girl named Christina. An Assyrian girl who was three years old when she was taken from her mother's arms on a bus by an ISIS militant. Then they forced the parents to leave on the bus without her.

My oldest was three years old at the time I heard about this. It finally hit home.

And I remember looking around and realizing that, over here in America, it's so easy for us to get caught up with the stupidest current events. It's so easy for Christians to get caught up talking more about Bruce Jenner than about our brothers and sisters being slaughtered. I've seen more rants on Facebook from Christians about the sexual immorality of our culture than I've seen about Jesus' Church being crucified and burned alive.

We're not commanded to rant about the sexual immorality of our culture. But we are commanded to pray for and visit and give to our fellow Christ-followers who are having their heads cut off because they declare that Jesus is Lord. Yet, we'd rather do the former and neglect the latter. Why?

I think it's selfishness. We'd rather get worked up about the things that offend ME rather than do the things that Jesus commanded us to do.

TOO BUSY FOR THE PARTY

There is another parable that Jesus told in Luke 14. He told this parable while he was at a dinner party, and he told it to offend the people who had invited him to this dinner party. He was at the dinner party with people who were chasing after the praise of men, who had a spirit of religious competition and self-righteousness, and who were too distracted to share God's heart for people. There was no humility, there was no sorrow for their sin, there was no care for the oppressed and the poor and the hurting. They invited Jesus to the party because he was the talk of the town. To have him over would boost their social status. First,

Jesus said to them:

> *"When you host a lunch or dinner, don't invite your friends,*
> *your brothers and sisters, your relatives, or rich neighbors. If*
> *you do, they will invite you in return and that will be your*
> *reward. Instead, when you give a banquet, invite the poor,*
> *crippled, lame, and blind. And you will be blessed because*
> *they can't repay you. Instead, you will be repaid when the just*
> *are resurrected."* (Luke 14:12–14)

Jesus first challenged them to not invite the people who can boost their acclaim and fame. Instead, invite the losers and those who can't repay you.

And then some guy says to Jesus, *"Blessed is the one who will eat at the feast in the kingdom of God"* (14:15). This man is referring to the Great Messianic Banquet that had been prophesied about for a long time (Isaiah 25:6), when the Messiah comes and ushers in God's kingdom. I think this guy feels a bit challenged by Jesus and is trying to change the subject. Because that's what we Christians often do when we feel challenged by Jesus—we change the subject and want to engage in intellectual discussions about theology. For example, it's easier to hide behind debates around, say, the end times than to talk about our need to forgive someone. That seems to be what this guy at the party was doing.

But Jesus knows it:

> *Jesus replied: "A certain man was preparing a great banquet*
> *and invited many guests. At the time of the banquet he sent his*

servant to tell those who had been invited, 'Come, for everything
is now ready.'   (14:16–17)

So another parable, this time about a banquet.

"But they all alike began to make excuses. The first said, 'I have
just bought a field, and I must go and see it. Please excuse me.'
"Another said, 'I have just bought five yoke of oxen, and I'm on
my way to try them out. Please excuse me.'   (14:18–19)

Notice that these are not bad activities these folks are
involved in. They're not busy planning a murder or cheating
people of their taxes. Nor are they angry with the man throwing
the banquet. Nothing about these excuses seem malicious at all.
They're just a little preoccupied with their new stuff. As we tend
to be, right? New stuff needs our attention, doesn't it? New stuff
needs a lot of time.

"Still another said, 'I just got married, so I can't come.' (14:20)

Marriage. Marriage is a really good thing. In fact, it's a *God*
thing. God instituted marriage. So of course this would be a
legitimate reason not to come. All three excuses are good; these
guys have no ill will toward the master. They're just busy and
preoccupied with other things.

"The servant came back and reported this to his master. Then
the owner of the house became angry and ordered his servant,
'Go out quickly into the streets and alleys of the town and bring
in the poor, the crippled, the blind and the lame.'"   (14:21)

The master is angry and orders his servant to invite the losers of society. Why do I call them losers? Because in the eyes of every normal person in that time, these were the losers. They could not keep a job. Could not contribute to society economically. They were the losers in everyone's minds. And the master says to invite them.

> "'Sir,' the servant said, 'what you ordered has been done, but there is still room.' "Then the master told his servant, 'Go out to the roads and country lanes and compel them to come in, so that my house will be full. I tell you, not one of those who were invited will get a taste of my banquet.'" (22–24)

Go get more people! My banquet will be filled with people! But those who I invited first, those who were pre-occupied and those who were too busy for me will not get in.

And the parable ended. That is all Luke records at this dinner party. Jesus told this parable in response to the guy who said, "It's gonna' be great when God's kingdom comes in and he throws the great banquet." But the point of Jesus' response is simple: the busy and the distracted and the pre-occupied, even though they're busy with good things—they're not going to be at the great feast.

Imagine how the disciples felt in that moment: "I don't think we're going to be invited back here again."

The servant in the parable doing the inviting for the master represented Jesus, going out into the world to invite men and women into his father's banquet. And those who want to be with the master more than anything else will come.

> THOSE WHO ARE CRIPPLED AND BLIND SPIRITUALLY,
> THOSE WHO UNDERSTAND THEIR NEEDINESS WILL
> SAY YES TO JESUS' INVITATION AND WILL FOLLOW
> HIM AND DROP EVERYTHING ELSE.

But those who are too busy, too preoccupied, will miss out.

ROOTING OUT THE THORNS IN YOUR HEART

Jess and I are reading a book by Francis Chan about marriage—*You & Me Forever: Marriage in Light of Eternity.* One of the premises of the book is that Christian couples spend too much time focusing on strengthening their marriages and are lazy about the mission of God that he has called us to as a couple. And the more we focus on that, the busier we are trying to make our marriage a happy marriage, the more we tend to be distracted from the ultimate point of our marriage—*display the love of Jesus and make more disciples.*

They address parenting, too. We can be so wrapped up in our kids' activities that we miss what the ultimate point is—to display Jesus to our kids and point them toward Jesus and help them become disciple-makers. We can get so caught up in what schools they should go to, what colleges they get into, what clothes they wear, what toys they play with—that we are actually lazy about our call to make disciples of our children.

> SO IT'S NOT THAT WE SHOULDN'T BE MARRIED,
> OR HAVE MONEY, OR HAVE FIELDS OR OWN OXEN.
> IT'S THE POSTURE OF OUR HEART TOWARD THOSE
> THINGS.

Are we too wrapped up in them? Do we see them as part of God's kingdom? Or part of MY kingdom. Do they exist for God's glory? Or MY glory?

Let me offer a few quick to-do's to help us not get too distracted and preoccupied:

1. Remember Your Union with Jesus

When we trust in Jesus as our Savior, we have a union with him that cannot ever be taken away. That union means we stand before God blameless and spotless; an heir to God's Kingdom; guaranteed entrance into his great banquet; His Spirit alive in us.

Remembering that union should free us. Free us from the need to make a home here. Free us from the need to chase after other desires. Free us from the deceitfulness of wealth.

2. Take Time to Commune With Jesus

A union without communion is silly. When we said our *I-do's*, Jess and I entered into the marriage union. But if we never communed, if we never talked, if we were never intimate—what's the point of the union?

If we've accepted Jesus as Savior, we are in union with God. But are we taking advantage of that union by communing with him on a regular basis? Do we take the time to pray? To sit in his presence?

It's in prayer, in our communion, in taking time out from the busy world, that God reminds me of what is most important; that he gives me direction about how to be faithful with all the stuff I own and people in my life.

God has recently led me to ask myself a certain question that may sound strange to you, but I do believe it's from the Spirit of God: *If I get hit by a truck in a year, will I be glad how I spent my time, energy, and thinking?*

And so it's led me to pray: *God, help me to live my life and manage all the stuff in my life—my house, my family, my marriage, my relationships, my role as a dad, my role as a pastor—as if I am going to get hit by a truck in a year.*

Out of our prayer and communion with Jesus should come clarity on how to be faithful with our lives in such a way that we use them for God's kingdom, God's glory, God's mission.

Are you busy at work? Great. That's not wrong. But don't be lazy about your busyness. Be intentional, see God's mission in it. One day you will give an account for what you did at your job—but not how much money you made for the company or how successful you were; instead for how much you cared for and loved the people you work with; how much you did it with a heart that sought to honor God.

3. Confess and Repent

Confess simply means to say the same thing as God does about something. It's to acknowledge the truth about something.

Confess to God anything that you have been preoccupied with. *Lord, I admit that I've been too focused on what people at work think of me. I've been too preoccupied with getting my house in order. I've been obsessing over shopping.* Confess it. Agree with God about the thorns in your heart. Agree with him that it is choking out the joy of knowing him.

Then repent of it. Repent simply means to do a 180 degree turn. Turn our heart's devotion from something and go back to Jesus. *Instead of obsessing over the approval of my coworkers, I'm going to rest in the approval God has of me because I belong to Jesus. Instead of finding peace in my house being organized and clean, I'm going to find peace by spending time with you, God.*

I'll leave you with this final exhortation:

Therefore, since we are surrounded by so great a cloud of witnesses, let us also lay aside every weight, and sin which clings so closely, and let us run with endurance the race that is set before us, looking to Jesus, the founder and perfecter of our faith.... (Hebrews 12:1)

QUESTIONS FOR REFLECTION AND DISCUSSION

1. In what ways has busyness dulled your heart and prevented you from wanting what Jesus wants, from seeing the world—and the people in it—through his eyes?

    _____

    _____

    _____

2. Are there one or two good things that you tend to regularly get too pre-occupied with?

    _____

    _____

    _____

3. What is a practical step you can take to enable your heart to line up more fully with God's mission in the world? Is it to spend more time in prayer with him? Does something need to be cut out of your schedule?

    _____

    _____

    _____

CONCLUSION

BE HUMBLE

Every danger we talked about in this book is rooted in pride.

The solution to pride is humility.

But what is humility?

Talking about humility is confusing because there are all kinds of definitions for humility. Some would make humility merely about external behavior. *Don't brag about yourself, be polite, help others.* That is what it means to be humble.

But we all know how easy it is to hide our pride behind a false humility. I remember being at a football banquet after my senior year of football, and I was asked to stand up for something so the coach could celebrate something I did. I honestly don't remember what it was for, but I remember the conviction I felt later that night from the Holy Spirit.

The coach asked me to stand, and I kept on eating, as if I did not want to stand. Then finally I stood up, and he said to the crowd "See, Chris is so humble it's not even a big deal to him what I'm saying." And in that moment God nudged me and seemed to say, "You have him fooled." Because, you bet I wanted to be recognized for my efforts. I did work hard all season and cared if people don't know it. But I wanted to appear humble. If I just stood up real fast and puffed out my chest and raised my hands, oh I would be acting pridefully. But by getting up slowly, putting my head down a bit, still chewing my food— I was able to appear humble. And thus garner even more accolades for my humility.

But then at the other end of the extreme is the super spiritual idea that humility means focusing incessantly on our weaknesses and our mistakes and our sins. Tim Keller, in an article for Christianity Today, wrote:

> We are on slippery ground because humility cannot be attained directly. Once we become aware of the poison of pride, we begin to notice it all around us. We hear it in the sarcastic, snarky voices in newspaper columns and web blogs. We see it in civic, cultural, and business leaders who never admit weakness or failure.

> We see it in our neighbors and some friends with their jealousy, self-pity, and boasting. And so we vow not to talk or act like that. If we then notice "a humble turn of mind" in ourselves, we immediately become smug—but that is pride in our humility. Humility is so shy. If you begin talking about it, it leaves. To even ask the question, "Am I humble?" is to not be so. Examining your own heart, even for pride, often leads to being proud about your diligence and circumspection.

Christian humility is not thinking less of yourself; it is thinking of yourself less, as C. S. Lewis so memorably said. It is to be no longer always noticing yourself and how you are doing and how you are being treated. It is "blessed self-forgetfulness."

Blessed self-forgetfulness.

But we're always attached to ourselves, so how can we forget about ourselves?

FOLLOW THE ANXIETY

In his later years the apostle Peter, one who frequently gave in to pride and self-sufficiency, wrote:

Clothe yourselves, all of you, with humility toward one another, for "God opposes the proud but gives grace to the humble."

(1 Peter 5:5b)

To "clothe yourself" is the idea of putting on a robe. Peter says to take off whatever pride and arrogance and entitlement that you have toward each other and toward God and instead put on a robe of humility.

Why? Because God opposes the proud but gives grace to the humble.

Humble yourselves, therefore, under the mighty hand of God so that at the proper time he may exalt you, casting all your anxieties on him, because he cares for you. (1 Peter 5:6–7)

God's mighty hand is the picture of God's strength, which delivered Israel from Egypt, which brought down Goliath, which did all those signs and wonders in Jesus' ministry. Humble yourselves under *that* mighty hand, recognizing how weak we are compared to him, how little we know compared to his wisdom.

And practically, what does this look like? It means to *cast our anxieties on him, because he cares for us.* This means we don't try to carry around these anxieties or take care of them ourselves. To do so is to be proud. To do so is to not trust in God's mighty hand. To carry around our own anxieties is the opposite of humbling ourselves.

To fight back against our enemies instead of trusting God with them is to be proud. To try to fix our spouse's weaknesses instead of trusting God to do his work in them is to be proud. To think we can control our children's hearts instead of trusting God with their conversions is proud.

Stay humble by trusting God to handle it his way.

And then he will exalt you in due time.

YOU KNOW WHAT "DUE TIME" MEANS? GOD'S TIME.

In God's time, he will exalt you. Not in your time. In fact, to give God a timeline is to be proud. To say, "Alright, God, I'll let you take care of this problem. But you have til next week." That is pride.

So humble yourselves.

And then he continues:

Be sober-minded; be watchful. Your adversary the devil prowls around like a roaring lion, seeking someone to devour.

Remember the movie *Jaws*? Once you've seen it, it's always in the back of your mind when you go into the ocean!

Well, here Peter is telling us that we have a very real predator on the prowl looking to get us every day, and we must be aware of it—even more than we think about a killer shark when we're in the ocean. We are to be on the alert. Clear-headed. Sober-minded. We mustn't get lulled to sleep; we can't get confused and foggy-headed about what is really going on.

> THIS LION IS CONSTANTLY SEEKING TO KEEP US FROM DOING WHAT PETER COMMANDED US TO DO EARLIER: HUMBLE YOURSELVES

In every situation, Satan seeks to tempt us to choose the way of pride and to not trust God.

The night of Jesus' arrest, just before Jesus was taken, he went to the Garden of Gethsemane to pray. And he asked Peter, James and John to stay alert with him. But Peter fell asleep. And as a result, he wasn't prepared when the soldiers came to arrest Jesus. What did he do? He took matters into his own hands. He took out a sword and tried to chop off the high priest's servant's head.

(Lucky for him, he was a bad head-chopper and only managed to get an ear).

Peter was not humble because he was not alert, and he fell to the temptation that this hungry lion threw at him—*take matters into your own hands!*

So now, 30 years later, Peter knew how Satan worked. When Peter calls him a roaring lion, he was talking about all the persecution and suffering around these Christians. The executions, the mocking, the ostracizing. Satan was behind them all.

And what Peter is saying is that this lion will roar—he will roar by causing hardships in your life. But he won't necessarily devour you. That happens when we react to those hardships in fear and by not trusting God, by not casting our anxieties on God, by taking matters into our own hands. That's Satan's ultimate goal.

For example, he doesn't just throw sickness at us. He wants us to rail against God in our sickness instead of continuing to worship God. And he'll whisper lies into our ears: "See, God doesn't care about you. If he did, he wouldn't let you get sick."

He doesn't just want others to mock you for your faith. He wants you to mock back and get proud, so he'll whisper lies like, "Turning the other cheek is for sissies. Don't be a pansy. Jesus wants you to be a pansy."

He doesn't just want to cause our spouse to hurt us. He wants us to respond to our spouse's hurts by taking matters into our own hands and hurting back. And he'll whisper lies like, "Your wife, she doesn't love you. See how she talks to you. You should find someone who appreciates you."

Some of you reading this are dealing with some pretty major hurts from other people—other people who have cheated you, betrayed you, let you down. Maybe your co-worker, maybe a family member, maybe a neighbor, maybe your spouse.

And Peter is urging you—*don't try to get even, don't try to fix the person, and don't close your heart to that person. Humble yourself and take the posture of Jesus and trust God with that person.*

And you say, "Well that's risky, Chris. What if that person takes advantage of my humility?"

They often will.

Trust God with that anxiety, though.

Remember, one thing that was happening among the Christians who Peter wrote to was that some of them were being executed in other parts of the Roman Empire. Some of them were being asked to renounce their faith or die, and for those people Peter is saying, "I know that for some of you the lion is roaring very loudly and very close. But resist him. Keep trusting God, even unto death." And some of them did die. Many of them. Including Peter himself.

But even then, Satan did not win. He may have killed them, but he did not win.

To use a football metaphor: we're playing for God's team. And the scoreboard reads a million to six because Jesus scored the ultimate touchdown through his death and resurrection. Our team wins in the end, but we must finish the game.

Satan, however, wants us to forget that God's team wins. As a result, his goal is not just to tackle the guy with the ball. He wants the guy who gets tackled to say, "Forget this, I'm done. I'm out of here. I can't run for God's team anymore!" Or for him to start attacking his own teammates: "You should have been blocking for me."

Peter commands us:

Resist him, firm in your faith, knowing that the same kinds of suffering are being experienced by your brotherhood throughout the world.

Now there is a lot to say about spiritual warfare, but Peter keeps it simple: Resist him, firm in your faith. This is not about holding onto mere intellectual doctrines. Peter is talking about a complete trust, a complete clinging to what we say we believe.

It's the difference between going rock climbing and saying from the ground, "I believe this harness can hold me"—and actually getting up 100 feet off the ground and actually trusting that harness by putting our full weight into it.

Peter's command is, "Throw your full weight onto God, knowing that you are not alone in this great battle. You are not the only one being tackled and knocked down in this game. Don't think God has forgotten about you. Remember you have teammates suffering, too. This is part of the package of representing God in this broken world. Resist the devil and keep trusting God. Keep casting your anxieties onto Him. Don't take matters into your hands. Stay humble!"

Then he ends:

And after you have suffered a little while, the God of all grace, who has called you to his eternal glory in Christ, will himself restore, confirm, strengthen, and establish you. To him be the dominion forever and ever. Amen.

This is not some weak God I am urging you to trust in, Peter's saying. This is the God who has dominion over everything. Everything! Including Satan.

HUMILITY, IN ITS PUREST FORM, IS TO BE SO ENAMORED WITH GOD'S BIGNESS, SO IN AWE OF HIS POWER AND MIGHT, SO TRUSTING OF HIS FAITHFULNESS, THAT OUR ANXIETIES—AS WELL AS OUR OWN POWER TO FIX THOSE ANXIETIES—ARE PUNY IN COMPARISON.

And that will protect us from all forms of pride, even the ones that are so easy to fall prey to in our culture.

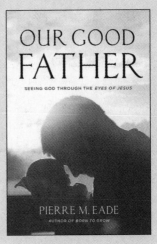

Pure Gold Classics

Timeless Truth in a Distinctive, Best-Selling Collection

An Expanding Collection of the Best-Loved Christian Classics of All Time.
AVAILABLE AT FINE BOOKSTORES.
FOR MORE INFORMATION, VISIT WWW.BRIDGELOGOS.COM

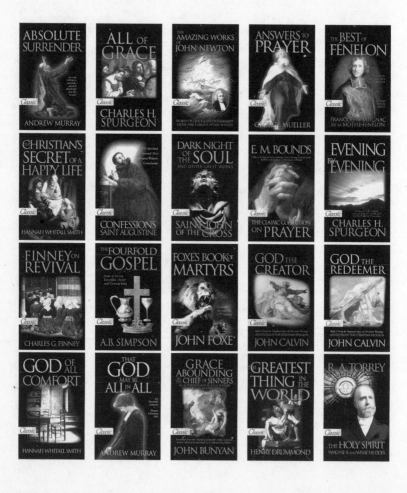